BLESSED
ARE THE
FAILURES

Hope for the Wounded and
Tear Stained Child of God

By
CHAD WILT

PRESS

This book is dedicated to my Jesus.
I love you and miss you more each day.

Table of Contents

Chapter One

The Anatomy of Failure

I have been a pastor long enough to have sore knees, bloodshot eyes, an aching heart, and serious scars in my back. On my long journey I have noticed a common strain of bacteria in every saint I have ever met, the strain of failure. The feelings of failure cultured by so many believers have never ceased to amaze me. Even more amazing to me is that there is very little spoken on the subject in the Christian church. If I have ever heard anything about failure, it shows itself as a three-second blurb sandwiched between endless hours of "encouragement." I believe in encouragement, I do, yet most of what we call "encouragement" today is little more than applying a bandage upon a bullet wound. Before we can heal we must be operated on. There is a tremendous need to deal with failure before we can even receive the reality of being encouraged. Encouragement is organic, it's the reflex of a pure heart, a heart free from the fears and sins of this life.

I am human, just like you. I hate to fail. To this day I love to win a game of basketball, chess, or to win at being the best dad, or child of God. Yet at the same time I have been freed from the false idea that failure is bad. This freedom I possess took a complete mental reconditioning that was often painful and unnatural to my fleshly man. What I attempt to reveal here in this book is the process of transforming pain to praise, and failure to freedom.

Failure is a four-letter word of sorts that is so despised by us as humans, that I am usually more ready to deny it than to accept it. Failure is not an option in life. It will happen to everyone, though we wish it didn't. We will all taste this bitter pill at one time or another. It is my goal to impart a different lens through which to view this ugly duckling.

For those of us who suffer from a passion to achieve a purpose and a destiny from what little life we have, failure is a beast made to be destroyed. For others, failure is just one more nail in the mental coffin life has offered to us. For all of us, though, there is something inside us that seems to know we have been created for something greater than what we currently have achieved. In an ultimate sense, we know we weren't born for failure. In a temporary sense, we had no idea that failure could lead to the ultimate victory that we were born for.

Growing up, in what most would call an inbred redneck town, my brother and I were fairly normal kids. We went to a small no-name school surrounded by other young no-name prospects of life, who would later on strive to escape the merry-go-round of their parents' existence. Some made it out, some didn't. Nonetheless, baseball was a local favorite pastime that parents enrolled their kids in. We were no exception. It seemed to be normal, and to have fun, you had to follow the tide. If someone tried to do something different from the status quo, he was a loner and also seen as a failure. Since we didn't want to be branded as such, we did the obvious: we played ball. Keep in mind we were in first grade.

Neither of us were very great players, but I seemed to fit in more than my younger brother. Not because he was weird (because he wasn't), but because even at this young age society seemed to lock him out for a reason I did not understand. Little did we know, we were about to experience the biggest curveball life has to offer, a debilitating pitch that often strikes out even the best of grown men and women.

I watched one evening as my brother played with his team. A classic set-up began to occur, the kind that kids envision when they are practicing alone. Bases loaded, two outs, ninth inning, and down one run. My brother was seven or eight. As life would have it, the lineup wasn't what the coach wanted, my brother was on deck. I know my old bro pretty well, and I could see the horror on his face even though he tried to hide it. The coach was yelling and screaming at the umpire, trying to get a substitute hitter. The parents in the crowd were expressing their anger and disappointment at the fact that my little brother was the next batter. Whispers from the stands were getting easier to hear. First blow, my poor brother was not wanted by his coach or his team. Winning became more important than the heart of an eight-year-old.

As the coach finally realized he wasn't going to get his way, he turned to my brother and tried to offer what bit of encouragement he had, which wasn't much. Fear gripped my little partner in life; both my mom and I saw it in his big brown eyes. With what little wind he had left in his sails, he walked to the plate, hat pulled down so low that it pushed out his little ears. With awkward-fitting pants slowing his pace, and dragging a bat equal to his own size, my brother faced the monster of failure. A David and Goliath scenario was quickly taking place. I only hoped for the same ending. Skeptical hope was in the air, parents, coaches, and team members hoped against reality. I probably would have done anything to save that little guy from that moment. But behind a fence that seemed like the enemy keeping me from my brother's salvation, I was forced to watch what happens to every life ever born. Inevitable rejection and failure.

Silence was over the whole park. Even though it was night, the dark seemed to be almost taunting. The first and second pitch, I don't remember. It was that third one that still plays in my mind like a video in slow motion. I can only imagine what it was like in his. With two strikes and my brother's confidence almost nil, the pitcher wound up for the last throw. It was now or never. Destiny seemed to hang in the balance. The ball came in low but higher than my brother's bat. In fact, his bat scraped the ground as he swung. He didn't even have the strength left to give it all he had. Strike three. Both teams erupted. One in victory and one in verbal disappointment. He lost the game for the team. The coach throwing his hands into his face and the dugout being thick with shaking heads, rolling eyes, and heavy sighs was too much for this little boy.

My brother collapsed under the weight of failure. He dropped his bat and the poor little guy just knelt down and cried. With chaos around him, the opposing team dancing in victory, and his own team forsaking him, the whole world seemed oblivious to the heart of one little boy. He couldn't even move. My mom ran through the crowd, past the coach, and lay in the dust with her little sunshine. I sat there stunned, unable to make it better for my best friend.

Helplessness is a horrible feeling. All I remember is walking out of that park with my brother in the middle of my mother and me, our arms locked, the two of us supporting the weight of a crying boy. He never played baseball again. In fact, many years later (almost eight), it took me about a year to convince him to even play basketball with me. He was afraid of the beast that killed his childhood. He lived with something no one could see. He kept it inside, ashamed at the limit of his strength.

Over the years, both he and I had similar experiences that brought us face-to-face with our inabilities. Some left deeper scars than others. I began to realize that as strong as I was, I did not have the ability to handle life. Being successful in an external way only temporarily numbs the continual inner nagging of personal "day-to-day" failures that we all face. What I often want, more than even wanting God, is to live without failing. Now, I would never come out and say that, but times in my past have proved me wrong. When I desire something more than God, even my personal purity, I have fashioned an idolatrous image that I worship. This is why failure is dangerous. Not because it is bad, but because it often drives me to religious perfection instead of surrendered brokenness.

Failure is no respecter of persons. Examine the heart of the sinner or the saint, and you will find the scars of failure that so often lead to depression.

Jim Carrey, the modern-day hit of comedy, said in the *60 Minutes* interview, "There are peaks, there are valleys. But they're all kind of carved and smoothed out, and it feels like a low level of despair you live in. Where you're not getting any answers, but you're living OK. And you can smile at the office. You know? But it's a low level of despair." www.cbsnews.com/news/carrey-life-is-too-beautiful/

Kurt Cobain felt what many won't admit. He couldn't handle life either. A list of names that we would not expect to have to battle the depression that comes from failure appears with a simple search on the Internet. Some of the people who fought, and still fight this demon, in one way or another are: Sheryl Crow, Rosie O'Donnell, Rodney Dangerfield, Harrison Ford, Drew Carey, John Lennon, Buzz Aldrin, Brook Shields, Ashley Judd, Vincent Van Gogh, Boris Yeltsin, Princess Diana, and Winston Churchill. There are untold millions of people who we deem as successful, yet they continue to wonder what life is about. Life and its disappointments are no respecters of persons. Yet so many of us believe that if they could only achieve the level of success that these men and women achieved, then we would finally be free from the vise around our hearts, and be safe from the prison of failure.

Henry Ford failed and went broke five times before he finally succeeded. Walt Disney was fired by a newspaper editor for lack of ideas. Disney also went bankrupt several times before he built Disneyland. General Douglas MacArthur applied for admission to West Point, and he was turned down, not once but twice. But he tried a third time, was accepted and marched into the history books. Babe Ruth, considered by sports historians to be the greatest athlete of all time, and famous for setting the home run record, also holds the record for strikeouts. Margaret Mitchell's classic, ***Gone with***

14

the Wind, was turned down by more than twenty-five publishers. Albert Einstein did not speak until he was four years old and didn't read until he was seven. His teacher described him as "mentally slow, unsociable and adrift forever in his foolish dreams." He was expelled and refused admittance to Zurich Polytechnic School. The University of Bern turned down his PhD dissertation as being irrelevant and fanciful. On and on the list goes, demonstrating how failure is only what we see it to be. Even in my little world, my third grade teacher told me that my ability to write was terrible and I would barely rise to an average level in life. I'm glad my wife and kids don't feel that way.

For some, failing is only the road to greater opportunity. For others it is the dead end of life itself, a place to stop, build camp and wait to die. Failing, for them, is the beginning of merely existing and never excelling. Besides the obvious benefits of failure in our journeys on this planet, there are some spiritual doors that are only open to us when we have passed through this painful fire.

I pastor a small church in the middle of nowhere. The people I pastor have issues, at times they are hypocritical and cranky, they have messed up lives, and are people whose children often count the days until they get to leave the house. They are argumentative and self-justifying, and quite often very prideful. In other words, they are humans, just like me. When I deny the fact that I am in need of something higher and greater than myself, I will only end up just like plain ole me again. I feel a funny feeling when I see myself or others only subscribing to our own ideals of success, yet trying to rise higher than we currently are. To admit our failure is to hold the key to real change. To be rebuked means someone actually cares. When I refuse to believe anything other than what I think about my life, I live in a small box with my name on it, and the only people who will be happy there are the people who are just like me, anyone else is not welcome.

Failure is a conditional reality that forces us to per-form where we are unable. This monster seems to have teeth that pierce us in the night: it invades the softness comfort of our pillows, the quietness tranquility of our morning cups of coffee, and the silence we enjoy when we gaze at our children, wondering if we are doing a good parenting job. It seems to steal all life out of life itself, and, if we are not careful, the fear of failing can often be all we end up living for in life.

Jesus said, in John 10:10, "I've come to give you life…" Yet so many Christians say, "Where is it?" Outside of the moment of salvation, many saints feel as if they only ever experience defeat and poverty instead of the promised victory for living out faith.

Failure, if not seen correctly, can only shape my character in evil ways. If I feel like I fail enough in life, I begin to condition myself to expect it. Let that go on, and I develop a strange twistedness of hoping to fail, simply because I have found comfort in the pity I can derive from others when they see me fall. Then, I might purposely trip just to see who is watching and hope-fully derive some comfort from them. This sounds crazy, but years of counseling has proven to me that this is the case with more Christians than I care to admit.

Many years back, a group of my friends went to go see a show late one evening. A particular girl in the group (we will call her Mary) could not make it. She complained and moaned for a bit about her dilemma and tried to get the entire group to cancel their plans. In her mind, if she could not go, we should have not gone either. Needless to say, she didn't have her way; at least in the short run she didn't.

We all headed out to enjoy the rest of our night and about ten minutes into our drive we got a call from Mary; she had an "accident." We spun the car around to go rescue our little friend. When we arrived, the scene looked slightly suspicious. Mary's car had slowly been driven into a small ditch. The car was barely stuck, and by looking at the situation, I gathered that she did not have an "accident." She drove the car into the ditch on purpose. I wondered why she would have done that and then, as she spoke, it all made sense. She made a statement about us not being able to go to the show now, and she sounded rather happy about it. I was not pleased; yet I understood that her staged failure was only to draw attention to her shattered and neglected life. She wanted us, since we missed the show, to spend the rest of the evening with her. Inside she was very needy, as we all can be, and failure tends to feed the need to be needed in all of us. However, God wants us to need Him as the solution/rescue to all of our failures.

Failure is the exposure of my limits. When I tell myself that my abilities far exceed my limits, I am unable to accept failure. Like a three-legged dog in a race, I often lie to myself about my real condition. But beginning to understand who we are and what our limits are puts us in the position to win the race with only three legs. I so often do not want to fail that I muster every ability I have to avoid failure, and when I do fail, I am more afraid to try again next time. I simply do not want to face the fact that I need strength I do not possess, for to do so means I have failed again. This is what the world calls a "merry-go-round."

For the world, failure is weakness. It is unacceptable and hideous. It is the wart on the end of our nose that needs to be removed so we can be accepted. We often view God as seeing us in this same way. "Be better and you will make God happy," "Try harder and you will do better next time," and "God loves good little boys and girls," as opposed to the bad ones. We somehow believe that it is our responsibility to take care of our own failures, and when we do, God will finally be real to us again.

Society often dictates what failure and success are. Ironically, those who hate failure often hate control. Yet they are succeeding or failing in an age where success and failure are often dictated by the majority of society, which makes them a controlled people. If the world applauds, I succeeded. If they shun me from the stage, I failed. If my wife accuses me, I lose. If my husband despises me, I am worth nothing. If my kids hate me, I am a failure. If my book doesn't get published, it's not worth anything.

My life and happiness at this point are conditioned upon the acceptance of others instead of the acceptance of God. I find myself asking, "How can God accept me when I fail Him so often?" The idea of Christianity has to go beyond God loving us. God loves people who go to hell, too. The fact that God loves us doesn't mean that we have apprehended what it means to be loved by God. Failure is a key part to having a positive foundation in the love of God. This seems very hard for me to swallow when my whole life I live on a pass/fail mentality. God seeks to remedy this.

For the world, success is temporary. It is only a matter of time before someone stronger, meaner, faster, or better comes along and makes you a failure, or at the very least a "has been." So, it will be our imperative journey to define what God sees as failure and what God sees as success, for if we continue to march to the rhythm of the world, we will only rise to the degree it will allow us to. Our lives will be controlled by a fallen, failed society, whose mission is to keep the train on the track of modernism instead of the beauty of individualism as a unified whole in Jesus.

Failure whispers to us that we are no good. It is the voice of hell itself. And sometimes we even hear it from others when it is not really being spoken. It is a hog. It can consume our whole life. Sometimes the beast grows so great that we find it impossible to process anything without it first being filtered through the sieve of failure. It produces such a pain in the mind and heart that often the body reaps the results. Hearts ache, heads hurt, stomachs are sick, and at times we feel as if we have a physical condition. For most, though, the thought of failing the ones you love is the greatest horror we could imagine. This is why, in my opinion, Christians face the greatest trials of failure of any class of people. Our faith and our relationship with God are based upon love. Not just any love, but love in its grandest form. And when we play the part of Judas more often than Jesus, we collapse in our own failure. Not so much because we have failed, but because of Who we have failed. To fail love is far worse than having failed oneself. To the true struggling saint, failing God hurts worse than failing anything else. We hate it, despise it, and tear our hair out in prayer, trying to pay for our own betrayal. When you love, you don't want to fail. But freedom begins to leak through my tough and calloused heart when I realize that failure was the final straw that brought me to the love that I hope not to fail.

As I grew up, my attention went to the stained glass windows of the church. I learned that God loved me, I felt this unconditional love, and I was enamored by God moving in my little heart. By natural process, the desire to please the one I loved began to grow inside of me. The desire to love turned me to the power of performance, to a desire to obey things I had not the strength to obey. So, I began to read the Bible, not because it was my new duty as a Christian, but because in it, I would find the rules I had to obey to please God. I so loved this Jesus who loved me that I wanted to do anything to please Him. This pure but distorted motive led my path down a grueling highway where my own strengths came up short and my mutilating attempts to perform God's will laughed in my face and scarred my heart.

I was crushed. I thought that this love would finally be my freedom from a failing life, but my eyes were still on my failure. I was focused more upon being a success than being a son who learns through hard things. All that seemed to have happened was that I had a greater desire not to do that which I was doing. Trapped somewhere between love and failure, I began to break and gave up hope of ever being free from me. I began to slowly understand the anatomy of losing, and never in a million years did I believe that God was the one who had me on this journey. In fact, for a while I felt the need to blame the church, the pastors, deacons, elders, etc. I turned against them because they could have taught me right, or they could have not hurt me. In reality, God had arranged my pain to bring me to the power of a resurrected life. Sometimes it is necessary to fail.

As Christians, the ideas, definitions, and ways of God should be sought after with all our hearts. For if we do not find them, we will substitute a cheaper definition of life and failure, only to become dizzy and disorientated by the effects of our personal merry-go-round of messing things up. If this continues, we will drill ourselves into the ground, digging our own grave. But there is great hope, for failure is a hidden medicine only God can administer in wisdom, to bring the brokenness needed to have a heart capable of great love. Truly, what I see as the anatomy of losing, God sees as the beginning of real success.

Chapter Two

Jesus...The Greatest Failure in the World?

Jesus. He is adored in many cultures and religions. Perhaps the most misunderstood man in history, Jesus is still a success in many cultures, groups, and philosophical circles. But Jesus is hardly ever seen as a failure. Yet, if we compared the modern standards of our society to the earthly life of Jesus, we might be surprised. Let's look at the earthly life of our successful Lord.

He was born of a virgin, but his neighbors didn't know that. Who has ever seen a pregnant virgin? But Mary stuck to her guns. She was innocent, though to her friends, she suspiciously looked like a failure.

Born in a stable. What king is born among animal feces? He was obscured for most of His life and He was forced to know rejection by friends, family and community. It was on this stage that Jesus emerged almost unknown into the field of ministry. No CD, no books, no authority from men, no backing of the church, no ordination, no financial plan, literally nothing. He then appeared to the world at John's baptism, a baptism for sinners. The Sinless One entering a watery death prepared for reprobates. Those watching weren't so sure about His credentials. If He was Messiah, why did He need to repent? Why did He need to be baptized? Jesus was okay with looking like a failure, He was fine with the masses thinking He needed to repent. He didn't seek permission from the synagogue, He had no finance department, and His goals were sketchy.

This was the foundation that God laid His earthly ministry upon. I'm not sure about you, but I would be a little uneasy about the whole sinless Man getting baptized in sinner's waters. I can see a committee seriously voting against a move like that. God tends to be ruthless with His reputation, and at times with ours. He calls us to represent Himself, and then how many times have we found ourselves acting a hypocrite and yet He is still not ashamed to call us His sons? God is simply not afraid of looking like a failure.

In the waters of the Jordan, the skies opened up and Jesus finally had His endorsement from heaven. The Presence, the Voice, the thunder in the heavens, the fire in the hearts of men! Surely, this was the kind of move that denominations are born from! Finally, the church would be born! Yet He walked away from any form of earthly success, leaving it all to go into a lonely desert, away from the crowds, away from the success of heaven's Voice, and away from all that screamed victory. On top of all of that, Jesus' only witnesses to what just happened were a bunch of sinners. Why did God not have the entire nation there to see and hear this? God doesn't care as much about His reputation as He does His glory.

In Jesus' life, he was misunderstood, despised by the church, hated, rejected, an outcast, a man of sorrows. In the loneliest times of His life, His friends denied Him, deserted Him, and betrayed Him. He was the underdog, a fish out of water, a Man of another world. He was slandered, plotted against, seen as harsh, cruel, mean, and yet caring. He hit people where it hurt, and yet promised them healing, He was a lover of the broken, the used, the abandoned, and the failures. He had little tolerance for religion and man's ideas of God, yet most of the world saw Him as just a great teacher. He died as a terrorist, an insurrectionist, He was rejected and spit upon by His own people, bruised, bloodied, beaten, and He never blamed them for their hate. This was how we treated God when He came for a visit. Then, He died. Bear this before the modern church and ask them who wants to be like Jesus, that prayer line will be rather short.

No church, no school, no Sunday school, no achievement program, no five-year goals, not even a decent plan was left. No book, no business, and no inheritance. On top of all that, those who loved Him most left Him. He literally died, in the prime of His life, as an earthly failure. His disciples didn't listen to Him, didn't believe Him, and finally walked away from Him. Not what I would call a great teacher, yet still today many see Jesus as only that. He left the riches of His life into the hands of eleven sketchy men.

When God came to the earth through Jesus, He taught us how to be human. He taught us it is okay to lose. It is okay to strike out. When the last pitch is thrown and we come up short, the Lord picks up the losers and takes them home.

When Jesus said in Matthew 4, "...follow me..." He meant, "Be like Me. Be okay with the fact that even I was seen as a waste of human life by the church. Those who follow Me will be viewed as a threat to the current status of success." But Jesus never viewed His personal failures through the eyes of defeat. Fulfillment of the will of God, no matter how it looks, is never a failure.

It was not until Jesus' resurrection that His followers really saw that this man was not a failure. Many times when we follow God and feel as if we have not achieved the victory we were called to, we begin to doubt. Some victories are not seen until after resurrection. This is why we are so encouraged in scripture to wait. Sometimes though, waiting seems to intensify feelings of failure. While we wait, our faith often takes the greatest hits.

Unlike Jesus, our failure points to a sickness, a disease that has plagued mankind since Adam. It is easier for us to create a religion that we can obey, than it is for us to take grace at its word, allowing our hearts to be changed by God through the implant of love. The late Rich Mullins, in his song "Hold Me Jesus" put it this way, "I'd rather fight you for something I don't really want, than take what you give that I need." Understanding that Jesus lived before us as a human and was seen as a failure continues to baffle us because we are still trying to be what we are not. Successful.

Matthew 9:12, "They that be whole need not a physician, but they that are sick."

It is only our failures that bring us to a place where we can embrace who we are without Him. When I do that, I check myself into His clinic, not because someone else told me I needed treatment but because I now know that I am sick myself. The hardest pill for me to swallow is that the medicine is free. Through failure, I am free to look into the mirror and allow God to erase the image the world demands of me, and I am liberated to begin my training. Within the limits of my power, I find the strength of God. God's original intent to lead us to fail is to reveal to us a side of Him that most never see.

It was dark. The Israelites were tired and hungry. Thousands were disgruntled, angry and disappointed. With Pharaoh at their heels, they followed God through a man named Moses, in the middle of nowhere. The pace was quick for the young and old alike, all moved with speed and anticipation. As they crested the horizon, they saw their fate. The Red Sea lay before them, mocking their escape. They had failed. Moses had failed. God led them to a place where they thought they would die. Anger flashed, blame began to turn viral among the group, and faith quickly waned among God's people. God showed the weakness of men to the enemy of hell, and with the taste of blood on their lips, the armies of Pharaoh moved in for the kill. But God was about to show His power. Through the perceived failure of one man, the success of God was seen by all. If I care to face off with reality, I am stricken by the truth that most failure is only perceived.

As I read the story of the Exodus, I often wonder if I would have been one of the ones who were looking for rocks to throw at Moses. When things don't go my way, a vicious thing tends to occur. I turn to a murderer. In anger, we flash at our brother without a cause, we loose bitterness between a forked tongue, and often become the very tool of division within a local body. A simple man trying to lead God's people through one of the hardest times in their lives, gets sour end of the deal. But Moses knew God in a way that the people didn't.

Psalm 103:7, "He made known his ways unto Moses, his acts unto the children of Israel."

It is a way of God to bring a man to failure. It is an act of God to deliver him from the failure God brought him to. So many times, we want an instant maca-roni miracle. Our faith tail spins into a direction that exposes our lack of restraint and character, causing us to see who we really are under stressful moments. Faith in God during failure is the power to part the sea that keeps us from the promises we often quote.

On one side of the sea, Moses is a failure. On the other, he is a hero. If I look deep into the life of my Lord, I see a common thread that I see in the story of the Exodus. On one side of the cross, Jesus is a reject. On the other, He is the ruler of the cosmos. Vision on the earthly side of failure is often warped with emotional fits that cause our friends to recommend to us a good therapist. But the eyes of faith know that the resurrected side of failure is the glory of God securing the victory of men.

What Jesus did in His earthly existence was defy all the current ten step programs to success. He submitted to His enemy and gained to Himself the victory over all. What man goes to war, knowing his enemy wants to kill him, and decides to win the war by letting his enemy crucify his body and disband his army? Absurd. But that is our Jesus. Too many times, we feel the weight of failure not because we have failed, but because we have willingly adopted a false definition of success. We don't wait long enough, I am often too quick to agree with emotion. Emotion seems real, but many times it is a passing fog that causes us to make the wrong turn in our circumstances. To stand is better than to travel the road of vicious emotion that leads to the destination of blame, self-hate, and feelings of failure.

It is always God's desire to put His people in places where they will shine. But when my light seems barely able to hold a spark, many times I extinguish the coal I do have with the tears of self-pity. Feeling sorry for myself administers a twisted narcotic that only masks the pain, just long enough to feel justified that I am not the real problem. However, give it a few days and the reality of who I really am sets in again. Substituting the Holy Spirit with self-pity keeps the part of the Godhead that is on earth at arm's length during our darkest hour.

Not only did God reveal to us a new definition of how to be a human, but in Christ He granted to us a new Webster's definition on what it looks like to succeed. Every martyr is seen by his brothers and sisters as a hero, but the world still sees him as a failure. Some people have little problem with this "dying to live" type of teaching that Jesus initiated. They sell their all, exposed themselves to hazards of all kinds, and then die horrible deaths for a gospel the world thinks is silly. To die for Christ is never to lose. These are the people of whom the world is not worthy. This is the ultimate successful failure. Look at Jim Elliot, who said, "He is no fool to give what he cannot keep, to gain what he cannot lose." Not long after this, he was speared to death by the Auca Indians of Ecuador.

When I am brave enough to uncover the raw meaning of salvation, I find that there is little room for me. The promise of scripture is that Christ will kill the old failing me, and bring forth a new and victorious image of Himself in the form and accent of the new me. This new nature cares not about failure. This new life I have received has come from the ashes of being a loser, so why hate losing? If such a glory of new birth can come from the weakness of men, what can the glory be of a man remade by the powerful hands of God? The possibilities are endless.

John 14:12, "Verily, verily, I say unto you, He that believeth on me, the works that I do shall he do also; and greater works than these shall he do; because I go unto my Father."

God sometimes has to leave to bring us to new levels. Now, I know that He will never leave us or forsake us, but at certain times our precious God will change the seasons and circumstances that make us feel as if He has all but left us to the wolves. But this "leaving" brings a greater power to do more than we ever could do before. James, John, Matthew, all of them had done some pretty awesome things at this point in the text. They had cast out demons, healed the sick, and brought the gospel to a hurting world. Yet Jesus refers to something else that they will accomplish if He goes through this failing process of the cross first. We often feel like if we can just get to the place where we can heal the sick and raise the dead that we have arrived, yet God hints that there is something beyond even that. Maybe it is the ability to finally embrace failure and really start loving ourselves? After all, what does it profit a man if he loves others, only to continue to hate himself?

The mind-bending love of God reserves the privilege for His children to do even greater things than He did while He was on the earth. By the world's standards, to be outdone is to fail. By the standards of Jesus, to allow us the power to do more than He did is the ultimate form of success.

My heart can't cope with such a selfless giver. To have the God of all eternity look at my failing abilities to keep His Word and then promise me His abilities and power is something that breaks my cold heart and fires the passions of the gospel in me once again.

What must enrage the heart of God is to see His intention for us to succeed through failure being traded for cheap, unfulfilling self-pity and self-punishment because we failed in the first place. The church today has lost the power of weakness. Why do I long to be so independent? In the beginning, independence was only the desire of Lucifer. Adam was never created that way. What I don't see is that my desperate attempts to please God without God's help, is to come to a place of achievement where I no longer need the One I was originally trying to please. It is a cheap and dirty pride that I use to try to keep failure from having its perfect work in me.

In Matthew chapter five, Jesus said that the beggars were the ones who were blessed. Those who couldn't even worship God without God. Everything in their life, mind, and heart was a handout from the Lord. This kind of faith explodes into harmonious prayers and songs of thanksgiving. Everything we have is a blessing, no matter how small, because it came from our Father. I often think about what heaven will be like and those who will achieve its greatest status. Impossible to know for sure, I am still able to ascertain that those who have the greatest gifts to give to God will only be those who had been given gifts that God gave them in the first place. Paupers become princes in the kingdom. Empty earthly hands are filled at life's end. What righteousness I have of my own, the Lord will not accept anyway, yet I still strive to have something that I can boast in. Paul said he boasted in his weakness. What I will want to give Jesus when I see Him, will only be that which was His to begin with. He wants nothing else but a woman who is as beautiful as He is. It is a wild and crazy proposition to state that failure, if seen right, makes us beautiful to God, a proposition that is wonderfully true.

Those who are branded as ludicrous, insane, extreme, foolish, and failures, just might have the heart of God wrapped around their fingers. To see an Israelite king dancing in his underwear before the presence of God doesn't seem like wisdom. Yet God was enamored by the humility of worship David was able to offer Him.

The law of first mention states that when a word is first mentioned in scripture, it has a tendency to set the stage for how the word is used throughout the rest of the Bible. The word "worship" is first seen in scripture when Abraham was told by God to offer his son as a burnt offering. Abraham had told his servants that he and the lad were going off to worship. The sacrifice of that which is closest to our hearts is more worship to God than a thousand songs on a thousand Sunday mornings. Abraham did in part that which God was going to do in fullness later.

Only an extravagant God would take His best and "waste" it on his enemies. Yet this same Being calls me to do the same. I struggle with this, not because I do not love this God who asks such things of me, but I struggle because I realized that I do not love Him more than the Isaac that I call mine. Isaac was Abraham's first tangible reality of escaping failure. This too had to be handed over to this all-jealous God. But when Abraham complied, God made him the father of many nations, of which I am a part. Obedience eternalizes the blessing.

My pride, self-pleasing spirit, and arrogance, ironically seem to be able to temporally free me from my failure (or at least make me feel better about it), yet most often times these things keep me spiraling into being more of a loser.

The children of Israel went around a mountain for forty long years. They failed and failed and failed again. The hearts of the people were exposed, their character found wanting, and their actions betrayed their beliefs; all because they didn't trust God with the hard parts of their life. Their unbelief robbed them of the success of failure. They never figured out God's ways. When I can't pay my bills, I blame it on the devil. When I can't quite understand the ways of heaven, it is the fault of another. When I am not being fed in church, the pastor needs to change or go. Yet it is often God bringing us into these tight spots of fire to expose our inability, so that we will trust Him and collapse in the strength of His previously gained success through the cross.

Is it such a bad thing to be at fault? Since when did the opinions of other men become so valuable? These same people, who I will not even listen to, strangely extract from me the desire to please them. This is a dreadful existence indeed. A co-worker makes me mad because I overheard them talk about how I dress. So, in a rage I blame, criticize, and eject them from my life. Oh, and I change clothes before I go to work the next day too. My enemy controls me at this point, and I am not even free enough to be secure in who I really am in God, all because of my offense.

Jesus understood the ways of His Father. He suffered, He was rejected, and He was by all worldly standards a loser. His death gave His enemies time to gloat over the perception that He really wasn't God after all. Their point and position seemed to be all the more fortified by the fact that Jesus died "unable" to come down from the cross. But wait long enough and every death will be servant to victory; every failure will yield to God's definition of success.

It is only when I have my ideas of how God is going to free me from my failure that I stay locked in this prison of performance. To let go and trust His sovereignty in the circumstances in my life causes my desires to die and His to live.

Will we let go of our idea of faith and freedom? Paul, while in prison, was the freest man alive. Suffering is hard, pain hurts, and losing doesn't feel good. But we are either born of another order, or we are not. There are either rules that we are governed by that do not make sense in this life, or the Kingdom is a scam.

It is time to rethink the life of Christ, for to rethink the greatest loser in the world lends weight to the fact, that in my failure, God is trying to put me into His good company.

Chapter Three

A False Victory

Somewhere between diapers and diploma, I have learned one thing well. I have been thoroughly educated in self-pleasure. I hold a master's degree in me. My enemies along the way were often those who failed to see my greatness, or at least failed to pay homage to giving me what I thought I needed. Sadly, this is all too common in the pulpits and pews of our nation.

Division in relationships often happen because my "I" is not capitalized by another. When we do not get what we want, or what we think we need, we get irritable and hard to be around. At least this is true for most, but not all, American Christians. Let someone with a fish on their car take my parking spot and they are an inconsiderate hypocrite. But allow me to get there first and somehow my motives are pure and I thank God for the blessing of a good parking spot. Arguments between husbands and wives often rear their ugly head because one or both are feeling like they are not getting what they want or need. Pastors are placed upon the firing line of gossip if they do not perform the way each member of their church expects them to. (The larger the church, the more impossible this becomes.) We have become a very knowledgeable people about our personal wants. But there is One who remains the suffering servant in our life. One who has a desire to be pleased that many times is not fulfilled. One who spends His eternal life agonizing in intercession for our lives. This Jesus who prays so intently for us is the same One who calls us away from ourselves so that we can come to Him. After all, in the end, the book of Revelation tells us of an angel talking to Jesus, stating, "all things were made for your pleasure and your glory." (Revelation 4:11) Funny, how he didn't use our names in that verse.

One of the reasons we as a people hate failure is because we do not like the way it feels. We have never really embraced the true reason for life: the pleasure of God.

Revelation 4:11 "Thou art worthy, O Lord, to receive glory and honor and power: for thou hast created all things, and for thy pleasure they are and were created."

Deep down inside, I know that I was created for pleasure. Maybe that is why we can be addicted to soft serve ice cream, cappuccinos, and barbecues. Why we need self-help books on appetite and addiction. We were born to both give and receive pleasure, but when our world flips upside down and we are no longer giving and receiving pleasure from God, we fabricate a cheap substitute. It seems that we must have pleasure to exist and when we do not receive it from my Father, we run to a whole pile of idols that will temporarily scratch the itch for why we were made. Work, schooling, men, women, friends, barbecues, money, fame, ministry, goals, dreams, marriage, sex, drugs, movies, games, alcohol, cigarettes, and millions of other things serve as my source for self-pleasing spirit. It is often the cheap things of life that replace the value of heaven. I can easily convince myself that these things are not wrong — and some of them are not — but how I depend upon them to give me only what God can makes them sin. My value does not come from my vacation or how I spend my weekend.

Some things in life are good, but out of order they can be destructive to ourselves and others. A father can completely ignore his family for the sake of making a living; a necessary and valuable task, but one that can become grossly overgrown into a murdering Goliath. It is my mind that convinces me that I am doing things for the right reasons, but that doesn't stop the sting from piercing my neglected children. Each man does that which is right in his own eyes (Judges 17:6), which explains why no one is ever wrong. There are consequences to self-deception, often a numb blindness to the fact that I am deceived. My beam has grown so big that I cannot see the pain of others, or the pain in my own heart. I simply reduce my world to one temporary fulfillment after another. Life becomes about running away from who I have become to gain much needed "peace." This numbness leads to a need for feeling, a need to be able to sense things again, a desperate attempt to regain the feeling of life. So the battle for pleasure continues as I feed me instead of Christ, at the expense of my family and friends.

Leonard Ravenhill, one of the greatest prophets of our time, said, ""Entertainment is the devil's substitute for joy." Joy is an odd and unfamiliar term for the 21st century millennial. It seems for most that the only way to define it is through the lens of entertainment. One of the first things that failure removes from our lives is the true internal sense of joy. If we continue to deceive ourselves with false definitions of biblical terms and truths, then we have no more a grasp on the things of heaven than the devil himself. Redefining joy, love, peace, and anything else found in scripture does not make the new meaning true, even if I am partial to the definition. Just because it fits my world view does not mean it fits in the Kingdom. I must tread lightly when I am involved in redefining the things of the Bible to fit my ideas of God. If I'm hasty about this, I might just be bowing down to my own "Golden Calf."

There are times, though, when my eyes are opened to the lens of conviction and I see that I have been pleasing myself more than God and others. This causes me to do one of three things: justify my position, repent and allow God's grace to change me, or to collapse in another cycle of failure. Sadly the first and the last are the most common. God longs to return true joy to our weary and worn hearts. Joy that doesn't need a date, a night out on the town, or a vacation. He longs to impart a joy that reveals who we are and causes us to rejoice in it. A joy that makes me happy that I am me.

In the Garden of Eden, there were thousands of fruits that God had given Adam to be pleased with, but it is that place in us, that place we hate, that seems to always want the fruit we were not created for. Neither I nor the rest of humanity were created to please me, therefore I find that no matter what I throw down the hole of self-pleasure, it remains empty. Joy still escapes me. Feeling pleasure for a moment makes us forget about our failure and tricks us into believing that, for a minute, we have succeeded, even if just a little bit. But for me to please that which will only be destroyed, that is to say my flesh, is only a temporary and cheap victory at best. Destiny happens when the real me and the real God collide. This is the ultimate form of pleasure.

As I went through one of the darkest times in my life, the thing I missed the most was God's living, breathing presence in the room with me and the joy that it created in my heart. In my mind's eye, as I look back over those days of failure and being exposed for who I really was, even the sunny days were gray. The memories are a constant reminder of where I can lead myself without God. The color of my life was painted by my own selfish hand; blacks and grays stole every beautiful sunrise from my life and left me wanting. I ruined everything I touched. I left a film of despair everywhere I went.

People were affected by me. I felt like King Midas. I got my wish and even though I had my gold, everything I touched died. Pleasure was not, nor cannot be, found outside of relationship.

I remember a day in my past that frightened me. When I was young, I had an urge to please authority. Affirmation from my dad, stepdad, or mother, was all I really wanted. When I did something wrong or was disrespectful, I got a piercing conviction in my gut that wouldn't leave me until I made it right. As I grew older and farther from God, I noticed that the conviction I had when I was younger had much less power over me than it used to. One day while arguing with my mother, I simply had had enough and I told her what I thought of her in a way I never had before. I spewed verbal bile all over her caring heart. When I was finished, I saw the pain in her eyes as she stood there staring at me in agonizing unbelief. When I saw that look, I expected to feel convicted. I thought for sure I would feel bad at how I had hurt her with my words. Then it hit me: I felt nothing. I wasn't sorry. I didn't even feel the slightest bit of conviction or shame. I knew then how far I had fallen. Before that moment, I would have told you that I wasn't that bad. Self-deception had choked the conviction right out of me. It took me hurting someone I loved to see the monster I had become. Sometimes it is the same with us and God.

I slowly began to figure out how I got so far from the love that first captivated my heart. It was simple, I did what I wanted to do and God began to grow dim. I slowly lost my vision. It wasn't an instant isolation, but rather a slow unnoticed, drifting, punctuated by nano-seconds of conviction that were so quick I wondered if they were even real. Sometimes when we are convicted about things that seem justifiable, it feels like those moments are moments of unneeded extremism rather than the whisper of heaven. Months went by and they eventually turned to God-awful years of misery.

No peace, no hope, no joy, no end in sight. Daily waking up under the umbrella of failure that kept me from the rain of God; I cried a lot. Tears of pain don't mean a change of heart, they just reflect to us our own condition, if we are wise enough to see it. I continued to struggle to escape my own revolving door, yet remained all the more unsuccessful. Daily routine only seemed to aggravate the wounds I already had. Frustration became more real to me than peace, and the lie more tangible than truth. To live and maintain some degree of sanity (which was highly perverted), I had to go to drastic measures for self-pleasure. It was only a Band-Aid on a bullet wound, but at least for a few moments I was escaping the merry-go-round of failure with the false lie of self-pleasure.

As time went on, I began to realize that I could not fix me. I needed God again, but I did not believe that God needed or wanted me. My faith, if it was alive at all, was comatose. I was in desperate need of a personal revival. I was sick of the treadmill of performance. All the praying I tried to do, all the Bible reading, the elders praying over me, the confessing of my sins, the oil at the altar, it didn't work. It didn't work because I was not really done with my tantrum of selfishness, and God knew it. I was lying to myself. I was tired of the pain but not the self-life. I was trying to convince God to let me have my cake and eat it too.

One day I was invited to speak at a women's seminar. Knowing the condition I was in, I refused. I had already been enough of a hypocrite in my arrogance, I felt it to be complete debauchery to be so in the church behind a pulpit. But, after a lot of pressure to go was applied to me by those who knew my condition, I reluctantly accepted. I was determined to be honest and state my failure and sickness before everyone. Maybe at the very least they would not go the way I did. I decided that this seminar would be for me more of a support group where I could expose my feelings. I determined that if I was on the way to destruction, then the least I could do was warn a few others not to go the way I chose. So, reluctantly I went.

When I arrived, there was a small meeting hall that was unoccupied in the building. It was the only place I found where there were no people. I was desperate to remain isolated, yet all I really wanted was acceptance. I was so depressed that even my sweat seemed to be infected with it. I feared to touch anyone lest my incurable disease spread to them. I was isolated and alone, by my own hand I ripped off heaven with my inheritance and I felt like a pig. I feared prayer because of how it had not seemed to work in the past. Lies filled my head so densely that they had me convinced that they were the truth.

Walking around in that little room, I finally let go, I felt myself go weak and I just collapsed on the floor and began to weep like a baby. God came into the room with such force and glory that a few ladies who had just walked in were instantly brought to tears and their knees by the presence of God. I simply told God from my heart, not my head — for I had tried that before — that I was done, and I truly was. I had had enough of me and of my own pleasure-seeking thrill ride that wasn't so thrilling.

When I submitted to God again and felt the pleasure of His heart wash over me, I knew that by failing myself I had only given God back His throne. He turned my mourning into dancing, and for the first time in years I experienced shared pleasure, God giving to me and me giving back to Him. This was success, this was the taste of victory, and this was joy! To think that all of it came through the birth pains of failure.

I died that day. The sickness that I had was incurable. So it is with self: it cannot be cured, it must be murdered. The cross became my friend and God once again became my Daddy. We are so driven to know pleasure that we have struggled for years to fit a square peg into a round hole. All things were created for the pleasure of God, and when I live for anything less, the cycle starts to spin out of control again, bringing with it all its craziness.

Love in its God-defined form is the ultimate cure for failure. When my parents, my co-workers, my boss, my husband, my wife, my kids, or anyone else blankets me with failure, I will not care if God's banner over me is love.

Following God will bring you to a degree of failing, but the ground of failure holds the anchor of faith well.

I have one life in which to practice faith in the midst of failure, for my eternal resting place bears no familiarity with failing. The rewards and successes of a life lived in faith before God while on earth will be the eternal reward and glory to God in heaven. There is no suffering in heaven, therefore there is no ability to know the God who can deliver from darkness and failure there. Only here can I embrace with opened arms the earthly life of Christ that often looks like loss. In heaven, we will embrace the eternal victory and pleasure of God. It is only my selfishness that wants here and now what God has reserved in heaven for me, for there are certain blessings that we cannot have until we get there. God wants to show me His power to part the sea, but before He can do that I must first be brought to a place of hopelessness, with impossibility at my front and an enemy at my back.

We try to reduce God to a controllable size and form Him into what we think Him to be, instead of letting Him show us who He really is. But one thing remains true: success is the fact that God is pleased, even if I am not. If I give to God, it is a token of love, for love always gives.

John 3:16, "For God so loved the world, that he gave..." When I give to God the way God gave to the world, He is pleased. There is one thing you cannot do, and that is out-give the Father. But His definition of giving is back-dropped with the sacrificial suffering of the cross, and the world says that it is unnecessary to be so foolish. God is pleased with us as His creation, but when we choose the unnecessary and give like Him, there is an eternal smile that breaks across His Fatherly face.

Pour your life out for the popular, and men will praise you. Put your arm around a drooling, elderly woman wearing a soiled diaper, and you will not hear the applause of the crowds. Giving in this way causes God's heartrate to increase. Yes, God has a proverbial soft spot for the least of these. This is why He has a soft spot for you and me. I was ministering at a nursing home one Sunday morning and felt the need to just be with the residents. One particular woman, who was poorly cared for, had eyes that were matted shut with a nauseating green substance. This poor woman was completely unable to assist herself in any matters at all, let alone having the dexterity to take care of her eyes. I prayed for her, unable to look away from her condition, and was about to go my way when God asked me a question. "If that were you, would you want someone to help you or leave you like that?" My stomach turned at the thought of scraping the snotty substance out of her eyes. I had to sacrifice my self-pleasure to please another, even if she wasn't conscious of it. I obeyed. As I gently applied a Kleenex to the eyes of this poor soul, the love and presence of God filled my heart like I had never felt. It was a feeling that cannot be explained. I began to weep at the love that God had for someone left to die in a forgotten home. God cares about us. He really does. In that moment I was the hands and feet of Jesus to a lady long forgotten. God went searching for the blind and found her through the smallness of my obedience.

As we carry on in life, we are liberated by the fact that pleasure is a good thing, when it is found in God. When God is pleased with me because of my life of faith before Him, and because I am me, He pours into me the ability to please others by bringing them to Him in hidden and often subtle ways. I am impregnated with pleasure as I trust God in my darkest times, instead of trying to do something on the outside to bring pleasure in. God puts His pleasure within me and lets it gush forth like rivers of living water to those who are without.

Every tree, rock, leaf, and expanse of sky seems more vibrant and alive after we have had an encounter with God. Why? Because at our return and immersion into Him and His presence, He is pleased with His Son in us and we see the creation that He made for His pleasure through His lens instead of our dark window of pain. God made beauty and was pleased with it, then He shared it with us. This is a Giver. When I see things as God sees them, I can only be pleased with His wisdom and I often shout in praise at the wonder and majesty of God. I become a wellspring of life in the midst of a desert that we often call the church. When we are pleased by God, we become skipping children again with a renewed awe at the ability of our Daddy. When we are enamored with His strength, we turn to simple childlike trust and we never fear again the lie that tells us He is unable.

Pleasure is the trophy of winning. But self-pleasure is not a golden faith tried in the fires of pain and failure. Rather, it is a viral depression that steals from us the desire to try again. It leaves us hollow and fragmented. We know that pleasure in its right use is not necessarily a bad thing. If we misuse it, the consequence is often a seriously dulled set of senses.

1 Corinthians 10:7 "Neither be ye idolaters, as were some of them; as it is written, The people sat down to eat and drink, and rose up to play."

Paul warns us of the dangers of self-pleasure. He calls it idolatry. Idolatry is the lifting of myself to heights that only God should be used to. Demanding that God serve my selfish desires is assaulting heaven with prayers that will never come to pass. Submission is giving back to God that which has always been His, and my heart is no different. He created in me the passion for pleasure, but He never intended it to be poured upon the altar of personal gain. We are like God in His ultimate form when we are giving to others out of a sacrificial heart that has been changed by Jesus. This in simple terms is what we call ministry.

A quick search of the text will give us an immediate view on the heart of God as He wrote to us about dangers of self-pleasure.

Romans 8:8, "So then they that are in the flesh cannot please God."

Romans 15:1-2 "We then that are strong ought to bear the infirmities of the weak, and not to please ourselves. Let every one of us please his neighbor for his good to edification."

1 Thessalonians 4:1 "Furthermore then we beseech you, brethren, and exhort you by the Lord Jesus, that as ye have received of us how ye ought to walk and to please God, so ye would abound more and more."

2 Timothy 2:4 "No man that warreth entangleth himself with the affairs of this life; that he may please him who hath chosen him to be a soldier."

Hebrews 11:6 "But without faith it is impossible to please him: for he that cometh to God must believe that he is, and that he is a rewarder of them that diligently seek him."

The fire on the altar of God is thorough. Place upon it yourself and your desires in sincerity, and God will birth in you again the desire to please His heart. There is one expressible quality that is common to those newly saved. They feel a freedom they have never felt before, and all they want to do is please their Father. This is what it is like to be in the family of God. Maybe you have been born anew, only to have lost your way? God is able to restore unto you the joy of your salvation. A salvation that was first based in His pleasure to save your beautiful soul.

God longs to give you a trophy, one that comes from Him and is made of things we need not to be ashamed of. A victory that bears no bitter end or unsettling disappointment. Yes, God longs to give His children something that will last for eternity: the pleasure of His Son in us. This is the ultimate intention for all failure, to end in the likeness of Christ.

So I must be vigilant and watch to make sure that I am not trying to escape my failure by pleasing myself, but allowing God to be pleased with who He made me to be; the image of Jesus His Son. After this I usually find that He showers His pleasure upon me and I am truly full of life and happiness.

Romans 8:29, God knew them (you) before he made the world. And he decided that they (you) would be like His Son. Then Jesus would be the firstborn of many brothers and sisters. (parentheses mine) Easy-to-Read Version

Chapter Four

Broken Rocks

P ain is the undesired womb of new birth. For a man to finally begin, there must be something within him that surrenders to an end. It goes against the normal cycle we have created, and it seems foolish to admit, but new beginnings do not come until there is an end of the old. To leave the womb is to enter pain. To walk through heaven's gates, we must first have our coffin closed on life itself.

A series of terrifying childhood experiences with the dark has given me a healthy respect for that which we cannot see. It is a small wonder that I am not afraid of it at this age in life. What we cannot see is what God is after. If I judge myself by my limited vision, I become either a scoundrel or an angel. God sees me as neither, He sees me as a son, which is better than both.

Before we got to the country life as I currently know it, my family grew up in the kind of area that you don't want your kids going into. This ghetto life that is often the focus of the nightly news, was my home. Somewhere in Houston, Texas, a mother and her two children were trying to punch out a living and stay alive while doing it. It was not uncommon to see the police at our neighbors' houses late at night, boyfriends of those who lived with us coming in and out all night long, men beating on the doors, screaming at someone inside to let them in. Creepy houses that would fit well in movies no Christian should watch, roaches the size of a man's thumb, things crawling on you while you slept, snakes underneath the refrigerator, rats that were commonly mistaken as dogs. Being dragged to adult parties by our babysitters (not to mention the beatings we got from them), knowing well the taste of alcohol, as often it was the only thing in the fridge, porno abundantly left behind by the Lord knows who, a strong sense of inse-curity, apartments with only a few bean bags in them for furniture, and a constant sense that always seemed to tell you that you weren't that safe — all this was the backdrop of my childhood.

Many of the experiences that swim in my head were the ones at night. Like the time we were sure there was a burglar outside our home, being awakened by an angry man as we all lay in silence, hoping he would go away, and being the only blond-headed white boy in a dark old house party where I had no clue where my mother was. Yes, often the hardest times of our lives seem very dark. But a great work happens there, too. God brings out all that we really are so that He may begin to work in our hearts.

Simon Peter was enamored by Jesus, as any new believer would be. There was a comfort from the power that Jesus carried that was almost addicting. A strength that called Peter from afar. Jesus, the Spiritual Rock, beckoning Peter, was familiar language. To Peter, Jesus was the ultimate Man. Yet there was something about Jesus that Peter knew nothing about. Jesus' ability to conquer the night.

Faith is a thing born and reared in adversity. The night tests what a man is made of. In the end, Peter knew this all too well. Peter was a man of strength and fight, a man's man of the greatest degree. Principle was important to him, and yet there was a side to Peter that was soft, if you got close enough to see it. It was upon this heart that Jesus cast His net and caught a future son.

All throughout Peter's life, he had a distant hope of being part of the generation that would see Messiah. But I imagine that he feared he would be like every other generation before him; they died waiting for the promised One to come. But little did he know, God had His eye on this old fisherman's heart.

Peter was familiar with storms like the men of the land were not. Many times he wondered if he would live to see the day. But in comparison to what happened on that cold Passover night, Peter would have traded a thousand nights in a thousand storms to be able to escape the storm of his own betraying heart. Peter was broken upon the shore of betrayal, but this brokenness opened him to a powerful victory. His story is a story of hope for the downcast and the betrayer. Those who have left God and long to return will find great comfort by peering into that part of the heart of God that Peter looked into.

Peter had to be strong. He grew up in a "wild wild west" of sorts. Roman oppression was around every corner, the fishing industry was hard work, and the very meaning of his name was not unlike the man himself. This is how we feel at times. Up and up we sometimes fly, feeling as if we can handle it all. We feel good about our family, friends, fun, and faith. We feel strong, because we don't feel like we are failing. We feel like Peter did when Jesus sent him on the journey to destroy Satan's kingdom in the minds and bodies of men. Watching sickness run and cancer flee, Peter felt at the top of his game. He was a follower of Jesus! Nothing and no one could stand in his way. He was confident about the feelings in his heart. Yes, Peter would stay with Jesus until the end, even if it meant death. He would never leave this blessed Lord, but Peter was so human he did not even know his own heart, as humans often don't.

Moments of my life that are interpreted by emotions, good or bad, are often the greatest times in my life where I truly cannot see. Blinded by feeling, I am no longer free to see God. No matter what victory, no matter what joy, no matter what healing, no matter what teaching or touch from God that Peter had, none were able to lift his sinking heart from the night he betrayed Jesus. All of his positive history with Jesus was swallowed by one act of betrayal. He felt like Jonah, and I know many people who feel the same way. The belly of the whale is not a home for sons.

The times of euphoric emotion seem so powerful when we are on the mountain, when the feelings are so thick that it seems you could almost cut them with a knife and pass it to whosoever will. These times seem so right, so spot on to what we think life should be like. We look at these moments and think that this is what it must be like to be complete in God. I have experienced many of these times, and I often begin to think that God exists to make me succeed. Times when my children are laughing and playing in the yard, my wife is happy, and the bills are paid. This surely is true Christianity. No, it is blessing from God that we should enjoy yet not idolize, for as sure as the rising of the sun, times will turn. This is where God wants us to know Him. The places in life where it is only possible for Him to move, bring Him the greatest glory.

This underlines a common but untrue thought in the minds of God's people. When things are good, they must be God, and when things are bad it must be the devil. The common modern thought is, "If God being good, and He is, then He cannot lead me to darkness." God is good, so good that He gives us good times in a fallen world. Yet it is we who often idolize those times to being more important than God Himself, and we blame Him when they exit our circumstances. God's ultimate agenda is not paying my bills and making me happy. His agenda is making me look like Jesus.

God loved Peter so much that it pained the Father to think that if Peter died on the Mount of Transfiguration that Peter would have stood before Him with a betrayer's heart. It is the plan of a great Father to sacrifice that which is good in the moment for that which is best in the eternal. On the outside, Peter was a success, but God, who looks on the heart, was staring at Peter's own self-confidence and desired to deliver him from it. Yes, Peter was heading for failure and God was taking him there. The greatest tool God has to form His saints often comes from hell itself. When I doubt this, I need to only remember the cross. This is the wisdom of God: to use a man to beat God's greatest spiritual enemy, by allowing that man to be bruised and beaten by that enemy. But within the bruises lay the final healing score. Satan zero, Son one.

Peter was about to become kindred spirits with ancient Job. Though Job lost all on the outside, Peter's loss came from within. Peter, like Job, heard the advice to curse God and die. Peter felt exactly like Judas did. Bitter tears removed the sweetness of former victory from the lips of this self-confident man. There was no achievement of Peter's past powerful enough to erase his current condition. Peter wished he were dead. He would give all the good times he had with God, all the healing's, signs, wonders, and miracles, if he could just be free from the heart that was in his own chest.

What we do for Jesus is and never will be better than Jesus Himself. Trade all the ministry and church life in the world for only Jesus, and you will be none the poorer. I am no different. When I fail, I feel the satanic urge to quit. Throwing in the towel seems like a logical choice, but if I quit, the life is ripped out of my guts like that of Judas. I hang upon my own selfish gallows.

God met Israel, when He gave the law, in a place of darkness. Upon that mountain, the fear and fire of God paralyzed the heart of God's people. So much so that ancient Israel wanted nothing to do with hearing God's voice. They sent Moses instead, and God showed Himself in thick black darkness. This God, in whom is the light of the world, seems to like the dark quite a bit. If this were not true, then why does God insist on making my life so difficult? A dear elderly saint was walking on a bridge and fell in the water. She said, "God, if this is how you treat your friends, no wonder you have so few of them." To quote Tevye from "Fiddler on the Roof": "God, I know we are your chosen people, but once in a while couldn't you choose someone else?" Every good saint has had the same thought.

When God was crucified upon the cross, He found Himself, once again, in darkness. Within the dark the law was given, within the dark the law was fulfilled, and within the night God can break those who have betraying hearts. Peter could not be broken by the sin of others, he could not be broken by the betrayal of Judas, Peter could only break when he saw himself, do and be, what he never thought he could do and be. An accuser of God.

While warming his hands around that fire, his cold heart was gnawing at him. Finally, Peter was so reduced that the opinion of a little slave girl sent him over the edge. Bear in mind that the testimony of women in his day was highly disregarded, let alone the testimony of a slave. Peter's need to save himself when things were bad was so much a part of him that he would stop at nothing, even betraying God Himself, to prove his innocence to a little girl.

When we fail, there is something that stands up within us to prove that we were innocent, or that our motives were pure. We scratch and claw at anything to make us feel like we are not guilty of what we just committed. We have to lay the conviction upon anyone or anything but ourselves. But God makes us face our hearts. If we are to be free, we must see clear enough to admit our crimes. These are mistakes we have made, these are sins, ugly, vile, well thought out choices against God, His Word, and/or His people.

When things like sin, drunkenness, divorce, death, gambling, addiction, and abuse happen to us, we can hardly see that we were meant to be leaders, spiritual rocks that would be given to the church as a pillar of righteousness. We do not see it because of how we feel. Walk up to Peter in his moment of betrayal and prophesy what would happen at Pentecost by his preaching, and through his tears he would chase you off and call you a false prophet. Peter felt nothing but pain, and though his faith was wounded deep, it was still alive. The prayers of God often are the only thing that will keep our faith alive when God makes us face the night. It was Jesus' willingness to pray for Peter that kept Peter from the fate of Judas. Today, many people are down and out. Their failures and betrayals are lifted to points higher than God Himself. But what they don't see is that at the right hand of God the Father, Jesus is still praying. Praying for you, that your faith would not fail. All you need to do is believe it. Let go and say, "Okay, God, I do believe You still love me."

The night tends to break the strong and the mighty. Why? Because God does not want great warriors, but little children through whom He can show Himself great. It will be a terrible humiliation for Satan to be beaten in the end by kids. This is the wisdom of God.

God wants to make men who will invade the night, who will no longer fear their own hearts and shadows. If I trust that God loved me enough to save me, then surely He knew I was more Judas than even I myself even realized, yet He chose to love me anyway. The fact that there is darkness hidden within that even I do not know about doesn't chase God away, it draws Him closer in that He might purify me from my own humanity and give me His.

It was Peter's faith, upheld by the prayers of Jesus, that led him to the joy that comes in the morning. Faith that Jesus maintained even when Peter could not. If God sent His Son to die for me when I was an enemy of God, how much more will God keep my faith alive when I face the night now that I am His son? Faith is the power to feel the kiss of God upon my forehead as I sleep. When the night is too much to bear, I rest in the arms of my Father like Jesus slept in the wave-driven boat. Faith is the ability to rest in God during my failures and trials, not my ability to generate good behavior while my life goes the way I want it to. Faith opens the door of God's acceptance when my mind tells me God has left me because of how ugly I am.

Certainly there is a place where we cease to be a Judas, and we no longer have that nagging place of betrayal hidden in the closet of our hearts. But first we must get through where we are, to be where God intends for us to live. Peter had to be broken. He was too confident within himself and his false ideas of who Jesus was. When I create a Jesus who does not suffer, nor calls me to join Him, I serve a Jesus Peter had created in his own mind. Peter did not want Jesus to fail, to die, to seem as if He had lost. Peter's pride and reputation were at stake, as are mine. Surely God would not humiliate me?

I recall when I met my wife. We were in Challis, Idaho, at a conference where some well-known ministers were speaking. I met her family and we exchanged addresses and the like. Her father was rather Jewish-looking, though entirely Gentile. Long gray beard, zit zits, and a look about him that was a cross between Grizzly Adams and a Jewish Rabbi. We went our ways after the conference and her father, clearly very interested in the Jewish culture, invited me to another conference in Cranbrook, Canada. I accepted and went to hear some of the same speakers again, along with getting to know her family better. I sat in a huge auditorium way in the back. I was video-recording the service for a friend of mine. The minister began speaking about Gentile pride and the need for us to humble ourselves to the Jewish people. He made his point so well that if anyone did come down to the altar, they would seem to be admitting that they were of an anti-Semitic mindset. Now, I have always had a soft spot in my heart for the Jewish people, for God still loves them greatly. I had even been to Israel on a prayer tour to pray for that nation. But as the speaker finished his sermon and invited those to the alter who needed to come, I felt God say to me: "Will you go down there?"

Whoa! Wait a minute, I was not anti-Semitic, and not only that, if I went up there, the father of the woman I was interested in might see me, as he was sitting on the front row with this girl who had stolen my heart! If I went up there, I thought I would be finished. How would the father of my potential future spouse (I had not proposed as of yet) allow me to marry his daughter when I was admitting to this sin? To make matters worse, I looked the part. My hair had long since fallen out, and tattooed scars left me looking more like a Neo-Nazi than the saint I thought I was. To go up there was suicide. Yet, God still pressed me. I then thought of how I must walk past all those people to answer this call.

So, knowing God's voice, I obeyed. As my foot registered upon every step, it left the auditorium with a strange echo. No music playing, and no one else coming to the altar, I was all alone in front of a lot of people. Walking down those bleachers was the ultimate trust in God for my future. But if I could not trust Him with this, then He could not trust me with His daughter. I made it to the front and knelt down to pray. Nothing. All I felt was the hard floor beneath my aching knees. I at least expected God to give me a personal euphoria of His presence for my obedience, but all I seemed conscious of was the pain in my knees and the heat on the back of my head from hundreds of eyeballs. Then a more terrifying thought hit me, "I have to turn around and face these people eye to eye to get back to my seat." Oh, how I wished I had sat on the front row! So I stood up, turned around and faced the crowd. Every person in the room was staring at me like a television at prime time. With my head slightly down, I tried as quickly as I could to make my way to the top without making a bunch of noise. And of course every head in the room swiveled and followed me back to my seat. By the way, there were only two of us who went to that alter. I often wondered if the other poor guy was going through the same thing as I was. It might not seem like a very big deal, but trust me, at the time, there was no problem bigger than ruining my future.

Yes, God led me to humiliation. Humiliation that I was not guilty of. This He did to Jesus too. Naked and bruised, He hung upon my cross. But before Jesus did all of this, God asked His only Son, "Will you go down there?" Jesus said yes to His Bride.

Peter was remade by his experiences. Instead of self-pity, he sided with faith. Instead of the demented payment of suicide, he believed in that one last look that Jesus gave him after he denied Him. Peter understood that God did not blame him, He blessed him with the circumstances he needed to be free. After that moment, Peter was never the man he used to be. Neither will I be the same, once I see that the limit of my life leads me to the unending love of a powerfully wise God, a God who uses the night to His advantage. The great King is the only One with power to beautify the negative that we continually face. But once we have gone through the gamut of defeatism, we will find a strange joy in our failing attempts in life. We will know by an internal way that God is with us. We will also find a power that we did not have before. The Peter of Acts chapter two is the Peter God always saw, and so it is with us. There is a chapter two in your life, the chapter that comes after the night.

God, for the most part, will not make our lives a continual sorrow, but mark my words, these trials will come. Some seasons in our lives are so dark that in our memory they are more powerfully familiar than the good times we have had. This life will fade into a glorious new one that knows no failure, no fatigue, and no night.

Let our faith not fail when the night comes to break us. But rather, let us trust the One who conquered the night.

Trials will come and go. Whether we are given new life or taken into a darker death is up to us, but one thing is for sure: the night never leaves you the same. Just ask Judas, and Peter.

Chapter Five

Busted Seams

What I am really made of often scares me. Often we feel so rancid within that our fear is God will turn His face from us and run. But it is strange wonder that God pursues the part of us He does not yet have. As sure as the rising of the sun, God no more wants our success than we want our failures. When we succeed without God, we act as if He does not exist. When we fail without Him, He is our first thought as we lie in the mud, bleeding. The life He envisions for us is a continual bike riding lesson with His hand on the seat, constantly guiding our journey. It is when I want independence, to feel as if I am worth something, that I will inevitably fall. A twisted idea permeates my relationship with God when I feel as if He will praise me for no longer needing

Him. The "happily ever after," in this distorted view, is me riding off into the sunset, giddy as a school boy, with God waving good-bye, wishing me a safe journey. Though this may be the mode of our current society, it is a vision heaven is unfamiliar with. Yet to continue to peddle harder to please my God ironically causes Him much isolation. It is the low and dreadful places where God is most real to us. When we seem to be leaking what little life we have left at the seams of our self-attempted surgery. Here we cry out well to God.

As any good father will know, the times he has with his children make that spark of life a fire in his heart. To be absent of being needed creates a vacuum that few survive. God created man in the likeness of Himself, therefore many of those feelings we have, that are often perverted and misguided, come from God Himself. God never intended to be alone for eternity. He dreamt of a created people who would be like Him, like in mind, heart, desire, and purpose. God wanted to put Himself in the position of being needed, and to need. He wants you. In all your failures, you are only the more beautiful when you break. We often quote the proverbial saying, "Beauty is in the eye of the beholder." Yet when it comes down to it, we really would rather feel beautiful to our-selves than to admit that God is crazy about us as He sees us in His Son. Do I really want to change for God? Or is it some insane itch of a dictator within me that causes me to only want to polish the idol of self? It is difficult to claim Christianity in all its beauty if you have not lost your own life. God will only begin in us as we stake a claim to our own personal end.

In Genesis 1:26, God says, "Let us make man in our image..." Knowing in all eternal wisdom what this man would do to Him, why would God ever create a being capable of such anarchy? God took a chance on Himself, He took a chance on love. Giving being better than receiving, God blessed Himself when He loved us as sinners. He still reaches to me today when I feel more at home wallowing in self-hate than in the fact that I have been redeemed. When we turned all of the principles of God on their heads, we began to live a life never intended for those who bore the image of God Himself. Living for self is a juxtaposition to God's original creation. In the prayer of surrender, I find the God I always heard about, and have even experienced, yet have never learned to abide in.

It is prayer, which is the place of conversation with the greatest being ever, that breathes into me the change I need to endure my circumstances. When I feel that God exists to erase the bad things that come to my life, I do not understand Him as Father. If God changes my circumstance, I remain unchanged. If God changes me, then it matters not my circumstance, I will emerge unshaken. This is the ultimate goal of a good Father, to bring about eternal change in His son or daughter. It is this place of prayer that enters depths that no man can describe, often after the pain that is equally indescribable, that I find God most comforting to me. It is here in this loneliness that God seems more man than mystery, more touchable than tyrant. In prayer, I understand that God understands, and this is where my trust begins to bloom, only later to bear fruit.

Prayer never seems as intense as when it is buried under fear and pain. It is when I hurt that I wonder if God really cares. Yet God seems to hear so much from us in the times when we are facing failure. Yes, like a straying adolescent only desiring his parents for what they can give him, we journey adolescent roads that lead to God only when we need the car keys to take us more quickly down our own odyssey.

"Lord, teach us to pray..." (Luke 11:1) was the cry of the disciples. They heard something in the prayer of Jesus that told them they knew nothing of prayer. Jesus, knowing the origin of His prayers, politely gave these ruffians an outline of what we call the "Lord's

Prayer." Beautifully, Jesus strung these words together to guide them as they began their own personal career of praying. What they didn't know was that prayer in its purest sense cannot be taught, it can only be experienced. What they were asking for were the right words to say, but what enamored them about the prayers of Jesus was not so much what He was saying, it was the pressure and passion in which He prayed. Upon Jesus lay the pain of completing the cross, so that the men He loved would no longer be damned to an eternal torment. It was this "Man of Sorrows" who prayed through tragedy and misunderstanding daily. This explosive pressure is what caught the attention of these twelve men. This pressure made His prayers addictive, almost alluring, and they wanted to pray that way. Little did they know that to be able to pray in this manner would cost them a heaviness of soul that often brings us to our knees in brokenness. Jesus knew that tragedy would strike the hearts of His blue collar disciples. This pain would then be released unto the Lord in the form of intense prayer. Until this moment came to their lives, Jesus taught them the best He could.

Some of the greatest times of prayer that Jesus ever had were against a backdrop of pain and death. The cataclysmic words of the cross, "It is finished," "...forgive them, for they know not what they do," and "...not my will but yours be done," were prayers prayed in the bloodiest battles of Jesus' earthly life. The blood at the base of the olive tree came from an agonizing prayer life. Yes, God knows that when I ask to be like Him, to pray like Him, to act like Him, that He must impregnate me with sorrow and joy to complete what others call unnecessary. At times on my journey I have questioned my sanity in asking to be like the Man whom the world hates. To live and grow up in the great American dream often puts a wedge between me and a true biblical prayer life. For me to ask for God's Kingdom to come is to also pray for the destruction of mine. When I pray this way, I am also shocked when things fall apart in my life. I truly have not yet understood what it means to be a son of the Kingdom.

A man attended one of our meetings. He was not alone, and there are hundreds who feel exactly like him. As the chit chat continued, he made the statement that his life was perfect before he got born again. After salvation, he lost everything, including almost losing his sanity. So the question is, "Is God really here for my wants and agendas or am I here for His?" Of course, the religious warrior in me confesses it is the latter, but my actions often prefer the former.

Looking at the God of the Old Testament and following Him through the New, gives me a magnified glimpse of the God who is willing to allow suffering to come to my life so that I will begin to seek Him again. Of course when I am suffering and blaming God, I fail to realize that suffering also comes to those who do not follow Christ, and yet these poor souls have not the promise of God being with them as they suffer. No, the world suffers too, and they do it alone.

The times in my life where I could ask for nothing, want nothing, and need nothing are the times in my life where I also pray nothing. Success is the cross upon which prayer is crucified. When I am full I forget God, but when I hunger and thirst, I am filled with God. Thus when I am closest to the Father, I look around and I also see my enemies. The most beautiful and poetic psalms of David were those in which he was pressed beyond comprehension. Life has a way of taking what I hide from others and squeezing it out into the earth, into the open where I could possibly be ashamed. But an amazing event occurs when the broken parts of my heart spill forth for all to see: the world smells something of God when I align myself with Jesus' sufferings. A fragrance only released through being split open enters the heart of heaven and the smile of God falls upon me like a life-giving rain.

The things inside of me are the things that often reveal the good, the bad, and the ugly. For fear of the bad being seen, we hold back that which is beautiful in us. Make certain, though, that the beauty that God sees in the vaults of our hearts is the weakness we feel. When I run to the altar, offering to God what I think is my best is disappointing, as many times God cannot accept it. The Jews did the same thing and their hearts responded, "...our righteousnesses *are* as filthy rags..."(Isaiah 64:6) The King James Version saved us a degree of embarrassment through its translation. A modern day equivalent would go something like this, "The good things that we do and offer to God are like a used tampons." Quite shocking! Those things within my heart, my strengths and abilities that I pride myself in, are the things that God despises. Yet the weakness that I feel I was cursed with is the beauty that attracts a bruised God. He died for weaklings, rejects, those who were picked last in grade school, the ones who always came in last, the ones who had nothing to give, and the ones that the world analyzed and threw aside. The fat, the ugly, the despised, the failures with pretty faces and scarred hearts, the ADD, the annoying, and the ones who can barely lift their heads for the weight of their childhood shame, these are the ones who heaven often longs to recruit. Not many mighty are called. (1 Cor. 1:26) If we have been enlisted in God's great army, then I have great news for you. You are not a mighty man or woman, yet this is the secret of your strength that the Delilah of this world has tried to rob you of. Being successful is for you and you alone. Being obedient is for all of heaven and all of the world as well. God's idea of a mighty man was a bruised, rejected, bloody, abandoned thirty-three-year-old Jewish man named Jesus. Might is relative. To God, a child in love with Him is the epitome of strength, success, and power. The same child draws out of us a feeling of "cuteness," but certainly not the image of power and might.

God beautified the ugly. He gave purpose and meaning to failure. He longs for the guts of my life, no matter how good or bad they look, to be laid upon the altar of service. This great Surgeon of the heart must first be allowed into the places where we trust no one, before He can bring His healing touch. To the wounded, God promises to heal by wounding again. To the broken, He offers more brokenness, and the bleeding He leads to the cross. This is the clinic of God. To use the very loneliness that isolated us to bring us into divine community. When we bleed on the operating table of God, we bleed with Christ. When we burn upon God's altar, we lay next to the Lamb. When we are broken, we find ourselves next to the Son of God being pierced on a cross. God's healing is that He has gone through it with you. The scars I bear inside that caused me once to question the presence of God in my pain, are the same scars that send praises from my lips to a God who healed me even before I was ever hurt.

The cross precedes all pain, wounds, and scars. Jesus was crucified before the foundation of the world, therefore healing was mine long before I even knew what it was to be hurt or abandoned. Knowing that God was hurt in my place before I was even formed in my mother's womb warms my heart to the love of God in such a way, I often find myself weeping at the thought of this Great Friend, who happens to also be the ruler of the universe.

In God we no longer have to fear exposure. Only dilapidated pride can keep me from the freeing power of being seen for who I am, a son of God. Though the world may label me as this or that, their definitions of me will go to the grave with them, and the name my Father gives me will stand the test of all time and eternity.

It is a sickening thing to think that we have learned how to shut out God and others when we were only created to be able to shut out the snake. When I turn my God-given abilities against God Himself, I am in a losing battle. The persistence that I have had in running from God should be the same effort I exude in striving to enter His rest.

The light of God has shone in our hearts and we no longer have to fear failure, exposure, and the jeering glances of men. When I know the God who saved me before I was ever lost, I bow the knee and pray with all intensity, "Thy kingdom come and thy will be done..." (Matthew 6:10) If within this kingdom I will have finally found my place and my peace, why then should I resurrect the desire to rebuild a kingdom of my own?

Wives, kids, bosses, co-workers, and all other relationships that used to show the worst in me are transformed by the awesome workings of God. I find that after I am raised from the altar of God, I possess a patience with others I never had before, a love that knows no boundaries, and also a desire for others to know this great King. Yes, the stuffing being removed from my life makes me more into the image of the beautiful Savior. After all, Jesus was an empty shell who knew no limits of measure to the Spirit of God. God empties me for the same reason, not to leave me hollow but to fill me with love, life, and His Spirit. May we praise God when He causes the seams of our lives to unravel and we are left standing naked before His presence.

Chapter Six

When the Church Hurt Me

When the church breeds more pain than love, it is very easy for me start a movement against the institution, and I find no lack of recruits. Thousands of us find a natural ease in locating both beams and splinters in the body, the leadership, and the organization itself. The sheer number of those who feel like I do gives a justifying satisfaction to my position. It makes me wonder how I could be wrong in trying to destroy and expose the authors of my pain. I often think up visions of ministerial grandeur centered upon exposing the wrongs that have been committed. I find raging within me a personal vendetta against the injustice, to the point of actual consumption. It becomes all I think about, and my pain and personal injury begin to define me. My mind swells around thoughts of saving souls from the church instead of saving them from hell.

Pain is consuming. It's a hog, an unnatural feeling that leaves us looking for someone to blame. It leaves us reeling drunk on the mistakes of others. My mind can get clouded and overcast with doubt. I find myself desperately reaching for any truth opposite to the theology that hurt me. I swing to the other side of the pendulum out of sheer rebellion against the misuse of truth. The image of God in my situation becomes like an abstract Picasso that is left to individual interpretation. In these moments I long for clarity, but all I desire is revenge.

Yet what I don't realize is that in my ministry, my family, my relationships, and my outreach, I leave a residue of division everywhere I go, even though I claim to preach love. (Though the love that I preach, would most likely seek to cover the multitude of sins that I am trying to expose.) I begin to boycott the Bride of Jesus because of the spots on her gown; not generic spots, but the spots that also tarnished my life. I can be so selfish that I do not care about restoration, the warrior inside me only wants retribution. I start to see myself as a spiritual superman sent to save the world from the "kryptonite" of the church.

If I slow down on my vengeful rampage, stop collecting followers to my cause, I may see that Jesus Himself caused offense to people in His life. Leaders will always disappoint. I have met atheists who used to be Christians, who walked away from the church because they were disappointed by God. If God Himself can produce such a pain and disappointment in people, then where does His minister stand?

If I believe the love message as much as I say I do, I would realize that the love I preach is not only for my enemies (those in leadership who hurt me), it is specifically meant for them. Why am I more willing to give love and cover the sin of the minority, to the poor, to the homosexual, but not the fallen pastor? Sure, I say to myself, "Oh, I am not glad that he fell, I am just glad he has been removed." This shows that I am not placing myself in his shoes. Would I not want restoration? Would I want everyone to give up on me? Would I want the online blogs to cannibalize what is left of me? Very quickly I see that I am hurting them as much as they hurt me. Often I will preach that we are not to fight fire with fire, all the while I keep my matches handy. If I am to be a son of God, I must look into the mirror and see that the spirit of my life has been dipped into the vat of bitterness and blame. I must begin to see that pain is a doorway to resurrection, not a trap door into offense and accusation.

It is not how I am able to process pain, but more about how I allow pain to process me. Like it or not, I must admit that whatever has been done to hurt me, I also have done to Jesus. While we were yet sinners, His enemies, and His accusers, Jesus died for us. I wonder if I would be willing to die for the man who betrayed me, instead of trying to build a blog to expose his errors. It is my experience that the Holy Ghost leads into all truth, and if I have seen the error of the theology, then I must rejoice that I have been freed from the error through the pain. At this point I am free to pray for the release of those who are still bound, not set my life's course to behead their ministry. It was pain that opened my eyes, and for that I must thank my enemies and praise God for them. My enemies have become my greatest teachers, much like Christ's enemies helped bring salvation to the world through the pain of the cross. The true desire of a Son of God in my situation of betrayal would be to sincerely and intensely fast and pray for their release, so that they too can experience liberation.

When I have had a revelation of the ugliness of the church, I must be very careful how I proceed. Someone else's failure can often lead to my own. As a leader, I can either cause more division or I can exhort others to unity. I can spread the fire or I can put it out. The book of Proverbs says that the Lord hates the sowing of discord amongst the brethren. Whether they are right or wrong, it is not my business. Jesus' command to me was to make disciples and preach the gospel, not expose those who do it wrong. I become mature when I understand that God uses donkeys. Sometimes I see ministries that I do not agree with, and instead of seeing the beauty of a brother who is trying to serve the Kingdom of God, all I see are his errors that personally offend my position. When my theology becomes more important than my brother who is in error, I am just as religious as those who hurt me. God in His perfect time and way, will strike the hearts of those who are wrong, and believe me, their hearts being exposed by God will hurt more deeply than any cheap accusation the church can hurl at them. God healed me through pain and He will often do the same for those who hurt me as well.

It's funny to me, as I have seen over the years many people severely hurt by a church or ministry and yet dozens, if not hundreds or thousands have been blessed and eternally changed by the same ministry. It is pretty arrogant of me to think that if this church hurt me then it is taboo for everyone else, too. I am not the savior of the church, this is not my bride, and I see clearly enough I should be able to trust God with what He calls His, even if I disagree with what He allows. Even if God does remove a man from a position, we should seek to be neutral and pursue the preaching of the Kingdom, not to continually find ourselves kicking a dead horse.

In Revelation, Jesus comes to correct a church that is wrong. Unlike me, He focuses more on the good that they did rather than the problems they had. He tells these churches ten things they did right and only one thing that they did wrong. He told them that they had left their first love. They had left the love that gave them the ability to bear with a sinful brother, they had left the love that gave them the ability to cover a multitude of sins, they had left the love that suffers long, that endures all things, that is not easily provoked, that thinks no evil, that does not rejoice in the sins of others, and a love that bears all things, believes all things, hopes all things, and endures all things. When I take this love into context with my pain, I have to wonder if I left my first love, too. Right and wrong are a poor substitute for love, likewise knowledge of good and evil is a poor substitute for the tree of life. Is what I am feeling and preaching bringing life? Or is it perpetuating the wrongs of others? What is the good news of that? That is a perverted gospel...much like the one that hurt me.

The Spirit of Truth in me will teach me that all men will fail me, and when they do, I should not blame them, but help them and forgive them. My time would be better spent proclaiming the beauty of Jesus instead of the ugliness of the institution. When I do things this way, people will be so attracted to Jesus that they will naturally pass on the fake.

One day while I was pondering my pain and the pain that I had caused others, I was reminded of the verse that says, "By His stripes, we are healed." God spoke to me and said, "My Son's scars remind the world of healing, and yours remind you of your pain. When your scars remind you more of your healing than your pain, then your healing will be complete." This blew me away. I realized that the wounds in my life were not healed. I also realized it is impossible to get off the planet as a Christian without ministerial wounds. For me to continually demand the perfection of the church was to demand an impossibility. My wife and I have issues once in a while, yet I do not run out the door to take my marbles and play somewhere else. We should not be this way about the church, either. I know so many people who miss a blessing because they won't attend church because of past pain. Yes, it risks being vulnerable, but without it I will never see the love of the Body. The pain I have caused God has not stopped Him from being vulnerable to me. I feel to be like Him, I must return the favor to my brother, who I can see.

So, when failure comes to me through stained glass windows and church steeples, I know that in that moment I feel as Jesus felt. But through the pain is born a resurrection, a new view of God and His marvelous relationship with me.

So, today I embrace my pain as an old friend, because without him I would still be in the dark. It was the pain of the cross that brought the resurrection that we celebrate. If I want a new resurrection in my life, I must be willing to forgive and embrace the unpopular message of pain. I finally see that it was necessary to be hurt by the church, for it was the only way I could really identify with Jesus. I no longer want to be defined by my pain but by the image of Jesus. It is time for me to love what Jesus loves, even if it means loving the thing I used to blame and hate. Love cannot be compartmentalized, it must conquer all.

We cannot allow our failures, or the failure of others, to taint the gospel we say we love. Trusting God with His word is amazingly hard for some believers.

But we are here not to expose the disciples of Jesus who are failures, we are here to make disciples of Jesus in spite of their failures. After all, isn't that what He did with you?

Doing unto others is never as important as it is when it involves being hurt by the church.

Chapter Seven

The Tree of Knowledge

We certainly do not begin our walk with God so that we can betray Him. But at times in our lives, we find ourselves in the position of the Last Supper. We feel as if God is telling us through our infidelity that we are in the mode of denial. We feel like we are the ones who could be the problem in this whole cycle of life.

The disciples were having a nice relaxing meal when their food got hard to chew after Jesus had told them that one of them would betray Him.

Every disciple left Jesus that night, but only one truly betrayed Him. God's definition of failure and abandonment are different than ours. Peter felt the sting of betraying God Himself, yet God never held that to his charge. Often what I feel about what I have done to God is not how God interprets what happened. Sure, Peter screwed up. He left. He sided with selfish desire instead of his sinless Savior. However, who we commit sin against has the right to interpret the sin however he or she wishes. God interpreted the disciples' betrayal as natural. They did not yet have the indwelling Spirit in their lives to keep them from running from God. Many times we hold ourselves to standards that God is not ready for us to tackle. He may be working on me in the area of forgiveness and I wish to go on to the mysteries of Daniel. When I step outside of God and His timing, I am sure to fail. This kind of failure is no different than a father watching his six-year-old son trying to exercise with daddy by attempting to lift a fifty-pound dumbbell. God does not fault us so much for failing but for not heeding our seasons and our weakness.

Recently, my little two-year-old discovered his rendition of doing pushups, which consisted of nothing more than getting into position and lifting his little rear end up and down on the floor. Not going to win any prizes for sure, but the desire to "do what daddy does" caused me to give him the gold medal for the day. Knowledge about what I am doing will most always cause me to believe that I have failed. If there was some way to explain to my little guy how to do a pushup correctly, then the knowledge of right and wrong would steal from him his daddy's approval. Through my teaching, he would realize his failure, and this is not what he needs at this point in his life. God loves us because we are His; He endures with us because He wants us to do what Daddy does. But God in His eternal wisdom knows that we can never be God, but that with Him we can do God-sized things. It is often my internal struggle to please God that gets me into the biggest sense of failure.

Back to the Last Supper. The Lord that night told His disciples that one of them would betray Him. Each one of them responded the same way. "Lord, is it I?" Maybe it was an intimate knowing of their personal weakness that caused them to question whether they were the one or not. Or maybe they asked because they didn't want to be the one. Nonetheless, all of them, even Judas, asked the question. As I thought about this moment in scripture, it dawned on me that all of them betrayed Him, yet only one was blamed. The disciples, minus Judas, were asking because they were not sure of their hearts. Judas was asking with the understanding that it was him and only sought to blend into the crowd.

God's definition is more important than any American dictionary. What God thinks is what is real.

Jesus never answered the other eleven disciples as to whether it was them or not. Because in God's mind, how could someone who had not the strength of God endure a God-sized death? The accountability that I often hold over myself only comes when I have been empowered by the great Holy Ghost. It is God's Spirit within me that gives me the ability to be a Christian. Jesus never faulted His disciples for their weakness before their spiritual baptism. It wasn't until Revelation that Jesus wrote some sad letters to the churches. Why? Because they had tasted of the power of God and yet simply refused it and walked away from it. The only thing Jesus ever really asked of His disciples before Pentecost was to follow, love, and believe.

The Garden tells us a lot about failure. Adam and Even had not the slightest clue that they had failed God until they were infused with knowledge. Knowledge is power, but more often than not, it is also an oppressive beast that does not have the capacity for weakness or mercy. With knowledge comes the ability to shut my brother out for his inability to do what I myself have done. Knowledge many times segregates people into groups, the successful and the unsuccessful. The reason behind this is because man was not created to handle the consumption of that fruit. God, however, being full of knowledge, has the ability to tame that beast, and with His infinite knowing also carries with Him the ability to tear down walls of segregation.

Knowledge is deceptive. It gives me a false sense of security and power. I love the quote by Abraham Lincoln, "There is nothing more ignorant than an educated man, if you get him off the subject he was educated in." Knowledge causes me to focus on what is right in me and wrong in everyone else. Very seldom do we see how we are abusing our abilities and our intellect; something God never does.

Jesus was the greatest source of wisdom and knowledge the earth had ever witnessed, yet this man had not a single door closed to anyone. What He knew did not keep Him from those who were lesser men than He. All were welcome to come to Him, and He would cast out no one. It is the Spirit of Jesus that gives me the ability to handle knowledge. The great Holy Ghost causes me to be able to bear the weight of failure, for the One who gives me the strength to carry the weapon of knowledge is the same One who knows how to keep me from using that sword upon myself when I fail.

Isaiah writes of the virtues that Jesus would possess as a man when He came to the earth. These virtues stand opposed to themselves according to the modern actions of men.

Isaiah 11:2 "And the spirit of the LORD shall rest upon him, the spirit of wisdom and understanding, the spirit of counsel and might, the spirit of knowledge and of the fear of the LORD"

Isaiah 11:3 "And shall make him of quick under-standing in the fear of the LORD: and he shall not judge after the sight of his eyes, neither reprove after the hearing of his ears"

Isaiah 11:4 "But with righteousness shall he judge the poor, and reprove with equity for the meek of the earth: and he shall smite the earth with the rod of his mouth, and with the breath of his lips shall he slay the wicked."

When was the last time you heard of someone who was extremely educated and prominent using their knowledge to live with others who are not like them? Oh, there are a great many philanthropists who will use their knowledge to help the poor, to send a check to the appropriate non-profit, and many other good deeds, but to actually live with them, befriend them, and get to know them? Don't get me wrong, we need more philan-thropy from Christians and non-believers alike, but we need more people like Jesus, those who will step down from what they know into being able to help those who don't. If all Jesus would have ever done for humanity was to send a check to the earth, we would still have the idea of a God who is really not concerned with our lives. When Jesus came to this earth, He was ultimately saying, "I care about your failures and I am here to do something about it." A God who will reduce Himself to sweating, defecating, peeing, getting tired and getting thirsty, alongside of me is a God who has my attention.

Mother Teresa was powerful, not because she cared, but she used her knowledge to help the poor and dying in an active, personal way. This can only be the power of the Holy Spirit. Man without the governing of the Spirit will use his knowledge to elevate his position in the earth. The more he learns, the greater the gap he creates between him and those who are unlike him. Knowledge was meant to be wielded by God. When man decided he would do what the demon did and be like God, he took upon himself a responsibility he did not have the strength for. So it is reasonable to say that when I do that which I was not created to do, I fail. With knowledge I judge my brother, I accuse my sister, and despise and blame my authority. When I do these things, I then realize that they are wrong and feel once again a strong sense of having failed. It is a God-sized work in me when I know of my brother's sin and only feel the need to actively help him through it. When I realize that someone intentionally hurt me and all I feel for them is pity and the need to pray, God has taken what I know and used it as only He would.

It would be safe to say that Jesus, knowing what would happen to Him before He came, and yet came anyway, would be a sign of the ultimate form of love. When He sat there in the room with those men the night before He died, Jesus already knew that they did not have the ability to keep up with Him in this divine war that was raging. Therefore, He never once faulted them for their inabilities. In fact, He forgave them before they had ever done anything wrong.

It is possible to come to such a relationship with God that we live on a retainer of forgiveness with those in our church, family, and friends. Before they ever do us any wrong, we understand their lives and positions so well that we release them from the hurt they have inflicted upon us even before they do it! If this were to happen in any church, that church would not only be unstoppable, but they would be one greater in atten-dance, for I would find myself joining. Sadly though, our knowledge of right and wrong is used well when we use it against others but many times we let ourselves off the hook.

I've seen churches split because of a controlling man or woman, the color of the carpet, and the sound of the music. All these things were based upon a form of knowledge, one decided that something wasn't right and instead of taking the role of Jesus and bearing with the body, they took the role of Judas and sold out the church to the demon of division. Knowledge puffs up, but love edifies. (1 Corinthians 8:1)

It will always be God's intention to use the fruit of knowledge to show pity and love, forgiveness and mercy. So many of us can find the ability, or at the very least the desire to want to forgive others, but sometimes we cannot find that desire within us to forgive ourselves. How can I hold something against myself when God Himself has released me?

Again, failure is often a tilted perception rather than a concrete reality. Even within those areas of our lives where we intentionally fail, there is forgiveness with God who understands all things. The reality is that I do not even know my own heart, so why cannot I trust the One who does?

It is right to ask, "Lord, is it I?" But it is not right to assume that even if it is you that you have failed. Each of those eleven ruffians needed to fail Jesus that night; they needed to be able to know a God who accepts them after they failed. Often times, God can only show us who He is when that which is opposite to Him shows itself in me. To know God as healer, I first have to get sick. To know Him as patient and forgiving, I must first fail Him like others did. Jesus did not come here to die needing the strength and help of His disciples, He came to die for His disciples who did not have the strength to help and to continue with Him. If the disciples would have been able to stand with Jesus in His darkest hour, nothing would have changed for Jesus. His Father had still forsaken Him because of our sins. If men stand with you and God forsakes you, you have nothing. If God stands with you and men forsake you, you have everything. Jesus promised to never leave us, even when we fail, even when we are the ones who leave Him. My heart quivers at these thoughts.

The knowledge of God is knowing that God is rich in mercy and forgiveness. Is He a Righteous Judge? Yes. Is He serious about our faith? Yes. Is there an eternal Hell prepared for the devil and his angels? Yes. Will portions of humanity be sent there because of their rebellion against God? Yes. But at the same, time God will release gut-wrenching sobs for every soul who ever slips away from Him. At times, my persistence in self-pity because I have failed must cause God a great deal of grief. He was tortured beyond recognition so that I could get back up and come to Him when I fail. But when I am made aware by the screaming in my mind of my failures and betrayals against God, I often try to take my own beating and punishment by self-inflicting a kind of cross experience that is horribly impure. I can almost see the Father and the Son holding each other, weeping for the souls of men who refuse to come to Him. You might think that is a little crazy, but the Bible says that Jesus is alive, making intercession for us in heaven. That means He is petitioning God through groans and tears for those like me who often persist in anger or pity because of our failures. God is so willing to answer the prayers of Jesus for our lives, yet He has bound Himself to not overriding our own will. It is me who keeps me from God.

Take some time and let God deal with you on these issues before you continue reading. See Jesus on that cross, making a way for you to come home, showing you what kind of a God He really is, telling you that it is okay to fail and that He is here to help us. God wants to live next to you. He understands, believe it or not, He understands. God knows, yet His knowledge does not keep you from Him, it attracts Him to you. Brokenness is the lure that enthralls God. Failure often brings me to the place where God cannot resist coming to my aid.

One day my daughter fell and injured her knee. In a flash, through her tears and crying, her head franticly turned to find her daddy. Looking this way and that, she finally located me. I was already running toward her, and before she knew what was happing she was in my arms. She never blamed herself for falling. She never felt like she had failed me. She only had the knowledge that Daddy was there somewhere and all she had to do was look at me. God sees you in the dirt, the blood, and muck of your life. Do you see Him? I promise you one thing...He is running.

Chapter Eight

The Fraternity of Failure

F ailure often brings isolation. It tends to remove people from the crowd. I know of many people who no longer attend a church because of failure, to one degree or another. As soon as someone fails me or I fail them, the tendency is to run, hide, and blame.

Adam knew a freshness of the Garden that we will not know until we get to heaven. But there was something within creation that was clean, simple, and reviving. If you asked Adam to describe fear or failure to you, I can imagine him tilting his head, narrowing his eyebrows, while looking at you as if you were from another planet. Yet as soon as he committed his famous dastardly deed, he was all too familiar with fear and failure. Adam's first response was to run and hide from

God. He isolated himself and it was God who had to come looking for him. At any point where I decide to start seeking God again, I will always find that He has already been seeking me.

The same way God combed the garden for his beloved Adam, I can see God combing the earth for His modern day Adamic equivalents. Yet we are hiding. Some of us hide behind leaves of religion, jobs, jokes, sex, money, hobbies, school, or just plain old self. The deeper we make the canopy of our defense, the harder it is for us to hear the voice of those who are looking for us because they care. I know of several men who are great people, yet they won't allow you to get close to them. Their defense is a well-timed joke. Everything is a joke to them, they can turn the most serious circumstance into a well-placed joke so as to evade the pressure. They hide behind the mask, never realizing what they are missing by coming out of the shadows.

God, when He removed Adam from the Garden of Eden, did not do so because He no longer wanted anything to do with Adam. No! God made him leave because if Adam were to eat of the Tree of Life, then he would have continued to live in sin and under the bondage of the devil forever. A loving God could not allow such a thing. But I am sure that Adam never thought that the supposed rejection he had from God was for his good. No, in fact I believe Adam thought that God had abandoned and rejected him, further convincing Adam of his need for more isolation. The male species is famously horrible about this issue. All marriage problems started in the Garden. Today, millions of men are labeled non-communicators by their wives. In fact, it has almost gotten so bad that women often accept the fact that men are "deaf and dumb," when the real issue at hand is the powerful force of isolation and fear of rejection.

Jesus taught us something powerful when He addressed unity. Every house divided against itself cannot stand. (Matthew 12:25) So with every situation of failure comes the pressure to leave, isolate, and run, thus bringing division and destruction.

I was at a prayer meeting at IHOP (the pancake house) one day, and after praying we all began to share where we were in our lives. A man who I knew fairly well, who was also famous for off-the-wall statements that he would later on connect with an explanation that would usually knock you off your feet, said, "I am in danger of the Amalekites." We all just kind of sat there waiting for what was next. We were somewhat used to the way he communicated. After pausing long enough for things to feel awkward, he explained, "When Israel was coming out of the Egypt and wandering in the wilderness, the Amalekites would often follow behind them and pick off the weak, wounded, old, or just flat disgruntled. Those that did not stay with the group got picked off." He continued, "Being with all those people in the desert where everybody stunk or was walking in animal feces, I am sure it was tempting to fall back a bit and have your own space, your own comfort away from the pressures of the group. I feel like I have been doing that, isolating myself from those who can help me." We all sat there kind of stunned. It is the kind of message a pastor really can't preach and be taken seriously. If he does have the boldness to say it before his congregation, it just looks as if he is trying to get his attendance back up for selfish reasons. But because this man spoke this as an average church-goer, it really hit home with all of us. The church today is in danger of the Amalekites.

When I do not have those around me to hold me up during the good times and the bad, I will often be picked off by the Amalekite of my mind. All of a sudden, in the narrowness of my thoughts everybody is against me and I seem to know every mistake and fault of those around me. This gives me the excuse to remove myself from them and do my own thing. Knowing about the weakness and failures of others gives me the right to hide amongst the fig leaves of life. It makes it easy to blame them and run. I feel justified to leave when the pain they have caused me is their fault, when in reality it couldn't be helped because more than likely it was just the confines of community pressing on me. It is easier to blame the church than it is to trust that God can work through it. It is easier to leave than to stay, reject than accept, shun than embrace. The ironic thing is that I am just like the rest of the people I tend to blame. We are all a part of the fraternity of failure. But instead of using those things that are weak about us to bring us to forgiveness and love, we often allow them to be the pry bar that separates us as friends.

I have had many people over the years leave the church. Some for petty reasons and others for reasons I was never told of. Nonetheless, what each of them saw were the things that were wrong, and this justified the isolation they ran to. Never mind all the things that were right. In the mind of the immature, a thousand rights will never outweigh one wrong. These people, instead of believing God to be big enough to work where they were, left. There is really only one biblical way to leave a church or a body and that is to have everyone in agreement that you are of such value to the kingdom that you would be of better glory to God to go somewhere else. To start a ministry, a church, or an outreach. At this point, the Elders bless and release you to another fraternity of saints (usually in some other part of the world or country) who are failures too.

I chuckled one day to hear that someone who had left our church was spreading rumors about a leader of our community who would "stand by the front door of the church with a shot gun, not letting anyone leave until the service was over." Bitterness and lies know no limits.

It is important to find a group of people, a church, a support group who sees themselves for what they are and who also allows God to be who He organically is.

Isolation keeps us from the cross, which is the New Testament tree of life. Running keeps us from the word of God, which so often God allows to come from the mouths of failing men. I often think of Isaiah chapter six, where Isaiah meets God as a seasoned prophet. Here you have a man of God who has spoken God's word to the people of Israel for years, standing before God Himself. At the revelation of who God is, Isaiah says, "I am a man of unclean lips…" Yet God used this dirty mouth to speak His word. Yes, God does not leave us there. It is His first desire to purify His people and their words. Yet, Isaiah's dirt did not stop God from using him before his lips were cleansed. At the first sight of dirt in the life of someone who happens to be a man or woman speaking the word of God, we disregard everything that is spoken because we see a speck in their eye. Even Jesus told us that we need to listen to the Pharisees, just don't be like them. But when someone's hurt or disappointment is bigger than their faith, it is hard for them to hear those words of Jesus.

Jesus created a community around Him, a fraternity. This band of brothers would later become the Church of Jesus Christ. It was within this small party of men that they found the greatest strength when times got hard. Peter would have never escaped from prison had not the fraternity of God prayed without ceasing for him. No doubt that those in that room who were praying for Peter's release had a speck or two in their eyes. Yet the speck they carried did not stop God from hearing their prayers for their brother. Why? Because love covers a multitude of sins. From God to us and from us to others, this scripture is true. (1 Peter 4:8) But when I isolate myself from the Body because they failed me or I failed them, I have no one to pray for my release.

I have lived in community for years. One place where I lived, I had my family, my brother's family, my parents, and four interns, all living in the same house. Try living with five women and two little girls with only one bathroom, not to mention the guys. Quarters as close as these will show everyone who you really are. But the value that this fraternity has become is priceless and has caused us to see where we need God, where before we didn't think we did. Yes, a lot of sin has been exposed, but how else are we to move forward? It is iron sharpening the iron of life that brings me to the prayer for more love in my life. Sadly today, as soon as the sparks fly, the church divides itself and creates yet another denomination. You will never know how selfish you are until someone challenges your idea of what is right. I will bear up with my brother until it becomes uncomfortable to me, or until it causes me pain. This is the thinking of the immature.

We had a lady come to us once desiring a community to be a part of. She spoke of fantasy and wonder as if the fraternity of God were nothing more than the happily ever after at the end of a deranged fairy tale. She envisioned smiles, slaps on the back, laughter, support, and barbeques galore. Of course, those in our group looked at her like a cow at a new gate. Quite shocking it would be for someone who walks into a body, only to realize that she has more problems to offer than praise, more pain than pleasure, and more misunderstanding than majesty. But why? Why does it have to be this way? God is jealous for one thing. Glory. If the church were perfect and without flaw, then we as believers and the world would look and say, "Well no wonder they are able to accomplish so much, they are perfect." But when we are far from perfection, God is able to show His perfect love through imperfect people.

Find someone who is able to listen and do not be afraid to give voice to your shortcomings. Often the honesty of one can break the dam of communication within the group. Yes, it is often scary to open up to that kind of vulnerability, but if we are honest we crave that kind of companionship. When I expose my own weakness there is something amazing that happens. Those with any degree of God within them begin to arise and to reach out to me in openness and forgiveness. It is as if when I pretend I am strong I am often judged, but when I confess my sins I am respected and comforted. Bring your speck or beam out in the open and people will no longer despise you for having it, they will pray for God to remove it from you. It is impossible to achieve your greatness as a Christian without a fraternity of failing saints behind you. You can only ride the wings of your gifting for so long before you tire and fail. But when God calls each of us to be prophets to each other, praying for each other daily, this is when we have tapped into a destiny that few find. When I daily immerse myself into this prayer life for my brother, instead of hurling accusations and blame at each other for our faults, we through prayer hold up the arms of our brother in battle when he is too weak to do so himself. You and I will never know who is there for us until our weakness is shown to our friends. Joshua and Aaron did not blame Moses for his weakness and inability to hold up his arms when Israel was at war. No, they became the strength Moses needed. When I hang out with the Amalekites, someone's arms are weak and I am no longer there to give.

Meet daily, weekly, as much as you can. Strengthen yourself and find joy in being with others who are just like you; failures who have found the success of their Jesus. Allow others to grind on you, allow the conversations to get hard and difficult, for then you will have the abilities of your love stretched beyond where you are now. Pain is often a good indication of an open door to grow. Let your maturity be tested and tried in the presence of those with whom you can find fault. Respond to them with patience and care. Be to them what you wished someone would have been to you. Forgive daily, minute by minute, moment by moment, and walk together. Forgiveness is not a feeling, it is a daily choice.

In the end it is we who must walk through the pain of fraternity. Not many people love enough to be exposed like Jesus was to their friends and enemies. Many in the church will talk about love, but what they really mean is just letting people do what they want so that no one is offended. The kind of love that costs your reputation and frustration with a brother in Christ is rare. Ignore the problems you see and be the solution to someone in need. Don't leave when things get bad. That just shows the superficial side of the church.

God's Church is and always will be a bunch of failing fishermen who manage to succeed in power to do those things that are humanly impossible, like loving your enemies, which at times means loving your neighbor or loving yourself.

Your personal Pentecost will awaken within you the power of God to love those who were formerly a failing nuisance.

Rejoice! Sing! Be happy that we are in this together and God has not left us. Sure, there will always be those who come and go for right and wrong reasons. But how we feel about them leaving, hurting, or failing us has all changed. It has changed because of the love of God through our hearts as human men. We are sad when they leave, but we are not stricken with grief, for we always carry in our hearts the knowledge of a God who never fails, and a brother in Christ who carries us beyond our fears to a fraternity of love.

Chapter Nine

Searching for the Why

The question "why?" is a very powerful provoker of thought. It is also the never-ending question. As a kid, I remember finally figuring out that there is no real answer for the question "why?" You can just keep going on forever with it. Of course I learned this at the cost of great frustration to my mother.

But the "why" of serving God is also often the revealer of our motives. What I do, will never be as meaningful to God as the reason why I did it. A Boy Scout can walk an elderly lady across the street for a merit badge and accomplish nothing in the eyes of heaven, simply because the motive could be selfish gain. The "why" of Jesus' coming to the earth was not seated in self-exaltation, it was rooted in a selfless giving to the desires of His Father. In the end, all things of a true saint are summarized in the betterment of God and others before the betterment of self. This was the life of Jesus, and so will it be the life of all those who follow Him.

When I was young, I was horribly plagued with lust. It became the backbone of my failing God. The knowledge that it was wrong only led to the further sting of guilt. Yet as much as I tried, I could not leash this beast. As the years wore on, I got more and more desperate about trying to beat this problem. Nothing worked. As soon as I finally seemed to have some direction or freedom, bam! It hit me again. Perversion drove me, and I hated it. I feared seeing beautiful girls at church, I simply did not want to defile them with my mind, yet sometimes I did. After a time, it became unbearable to live with myself. I made brash and self-destructive promises to God, only to break every one of them.

After years of confessing, deliverance, prayer, and attempted obedience that didn't work, God revealed to me my motive. In the gentlest way, He spoke to me, not so much in these exact words but with the same point: "Chad, you want to be free for the wrong reasons. You simply can't stand to see yourself like this. You want to be free from lust more than you want Me. Your prayers have been consumed with this one issue, you have lost your ability to praise Me and worship Me for who I am regardless of who you are. Lust has become your entire focus and in some strange way I exist only to free you from this sin. You have forgotten Me, My power, and My glory. You are in this for you, to make yourself feel better about yourself. My freedom is not for you to feel better about yourself, it is for My glory. Will you serve Me for the rest of your life even if I leave you with this problem?"

I sat stunned. In a moment, I realized how selfish I had become, and that I had reduced God down to a bottle of medicine that I ran to when I felt sick, only to put Him back on the shelf when the selfish nausea had temporarily subsided. I was smitten in my heart. I began to see how I had not trusted my Father with my failure. My eyes were opening to the wonder of God's mystery. The mystery that He was in me regardless of my failures. I had made a god out of my freedom and I was asking God to give me strength to bow to this hideous idol. No wonder I battled it for so long. I was too stubborn and deaf to God's voice for me concerning my situation. I was too busy trying to be good enough for my daddy that I missed loving Him.

I remember praying one day the prayer that Paris Reidhead prayed in his famous sermon, "Ten shekels and a shirt." This was the prayer that changed my life again. "God, I will serve you all the rest of my days, even if you send me to hell at the end of it all I will still serve you because you are worthy. I am not making a deal with you. I am yours whether you free me from me or not." After praying this, God moved so deeply in my heart that everything changed. My "why" was set right, and therefore everything else began to come into alignment with God. (Of course I knew in my heart that if I served God for God alone, at the end of all time He would not send me to hell, but it was the fact that I was no longer serving God for me anymore, that was the power behind the prayer.)

After this, I began to thank God for every moment, even when I would jump into sin. (Because we never "fall" into sin, we usually jump right in.) I thanked Him for saving me and making me His and that I was no longer the property of the devil. I will not lie, there was a battle in my mind. The enemy would tell me that I was a hypocrite for believing I was free from lust and right with God. The devil had some validity to his lie because I had just finished enjoying the sin of lust in my body. But I chose to believe God instead of my sin, and I wasn't alive anymore to be free from iniquity, I was alive to serve the living God. A strange thing happened.

I cannot tell you the day nor the hour that I was freed from lust because I was not focusing on it anymore. But one day I realized that I was no longer failing in this area of my life. I was happy to realize this of course, but I was happier to be a child of the King. I relied upon His grace and power to do with me as He saw best, and once my "why" of serving Him was set straight, He gave the freedom I once sought.

God is jealous, He does not want to be served for what He can do, He wants to be served for who He is. Though He can do a great many things, I must never reduce Him to a cosmic table waiter who only exists to fill my fancy.

Why do you want to be free from failure? Is it for the glory of your God? Is it because Jesus Christ suffered and died to have all of you? Or is it because you are tired of being seen as the heel? Is it because you are tired of living with you? Or that you are tired of not matching up to the standards of society and you decided to try God to see if He could liberate you? Whatever the reason, it must not be self-centered. If there is not some place in your heart that you have come to peace with in trusting God where you are at and not asking for release, you might consider re-evaluating your motives.

If you find that you are self-centered in desire, you can be sure of one thing, you will remain as you are.

Being saved from hell is a byproduct of salvation. Being saved from self is also a byproduct of God's accomplishments upon the cross. The prime product of the saving grace of God is a restored relationship between God and His children. Gaining the oneness that we lost in the Garden is God's ultimate desire, for it is only in this unity that He can be glorified and His pleasure is the center for all things that exist.

I had come to a place in my life where I was so in love with God that nothing else mattered. I had made the decision to stay single and be free to serve the Lord. I tried to take Paul literally when he said it was better for a man to remain as he was. The Word was very important to me and I was willing to make that sacrifice for Jesus. Before all of this though, marriage was a constant torment to me. I wanted to be married and I was too afraid to allow that desire to pass through God's holy fire, because I was worried that God would ask me to remain single. So I never prayed about it. I often ignored God on that issue so that I would not have to hear His answer. I knew I was being selfish and not really truly desiring His will to be done. But all that changed after God captured my heart in a deeper way.

I finally laid it all down and did not care. I felt so free! Like I finally had direction in my life and I was released to pursue it! It was settled, I would stay single and serve the gospel. Then a funny thing started to occur.

Authorities in my life kept coming to me and telling me that God was going to send me a wife. I could not get away from the nagging of God. Everywhere I turned in scripture, it was about a wife, and it drove me nuts. I must admit I was angry. I had spent all those years battling this desire, I finally give it up and I loved God more than anyone and He sends me a bride? How could He do this to me? This, to me, was the epitome of not being fair.

After some time, I began to look at my "why" again. I was slowly opened to the thought that if God had given me a wife before I had laid her down, then in a sense God would have given me another idol to worship. I remember Him speaking to me one day something like this, "Chad, I now can trust you with what is Mine. You may call her your wife, but she is and always will be My daughter. Before you laid her upon My altar, you would have substituted Me for her, much like Adam did. But you laid your Isaac upon the altar, and I am returning her to you." After hearing this, I understood the wisdom of a Father. The Father of my bride was seeking not only my eternal and marital welfare, but his daughter's. The wisdom of heaven's throne, in one swift move, not only secured to itself my heart, but also the safety of a girl God had created. God fixed my "why" without me knowing it. Had I not allowed Him to, I would have failed. Yes, He could have worked with it, but failure is not supposed to be the consistent norm of our lives. It is only to bring us to a place in Christ where priorities are aligned and God sits unchallenged upon the throne of our hearts, minds, bodies, and vocations. Once He really and truly reigns supreme in us, then He can begin guiding us by a different leader, one not called failure.

Why? Why do we want to be free from failure? Is it for Him or us? He knows already the "why." It is up to me to be honest enough to meet God squarely and truly. If I allow Him to touch the "why" of my life, everything else will fall into place. Seek first the kingdom of God... the rest will be taken care of.

The other form of "why" comes when I demand answers from God that He usually never intends to answer. When I get grumpy with God, I often feel like He made a mistake concerning the pain I have had to endure, and I seek answers to vent my disappointment. Sovereignty takes great faith to believe in. When I am drinking coffee with my friends, discussing the things of God, sovereignty is a great topic, but when the same subject is applied to my misfortune I find it much less palatable.

Over the years, as a pastor, I have watched many people excel and suffer defeat. The one true difference between the two was not the severity of the circumstances but the faith applied to God's sovereignty in them. I have personally witnessed people coming out of rape, satanic ritual abuse, schizophrenia, and many other horrible things to emerge not only victorious, but also to stand up to lead others out of the same darkness. At the same time, I have watched people's entire faith be destroyed because of offense over minor relationship issues. The difference between the two was the first one cared not about what they must suffer for Christ as long as they gained Him, and the latter was more interested in God being a means to their own end. I have found in my own life that if I wait long enough, all the "whys" go away. The individual moments of our lives can never define the whole, yet this is what most people fall prey to. Painful moments cannot be the hinge upon which our entire life swings. We sometimes must refrain from asking "why?" and wait until God shows His purpose. This process brings about a self-crucifixion that makes us more like Jesus. It is also a gospel that is not popular.

Be assured that all motives of our lives will be exposed on the final day. God simply longs to purify not only our lives, but our own personal "why" of serving God, our "why" of being free, and our "why" of being in ministry. Love is the laying down of our lives for our friends. This same love must be showed to God when we feel as if He has betrayed us. To do this takes great faith, but this faith will yield itself into an amazing eternal reward.

When I feel like I am getting the short end of the stick, I often think of Paul. He was beaten over 300 times. He was shipwrecked twice, having his skin pickled in saltwater while being in danger of the massive sharks that hunted those waters. He was rejected, abandoned by his followers, at times without clothes, hungry, distressed, afraid, in danger amongst robbers, in danger from his own people, in danger of the Romans, and in the end never got to fulfill his dream of going to Spain. Very disappointing, considering that you spend your whole life for a God who treats you like this. Yet Paul counted it a joy to fill up that which was lacking in the church. (Colossians. 1:24) Suffering is not popular, yet it is what separates the mature from the immature. Every person in the Bible who changed a nation or a culture, male or female, underwent a massive form of suffering. But they also emerged with a massive form of power. God promises to make every cross bow before resurrection, every imprisonment to bow before becoming a ruler, and every pit to bow before praise. Christians simply do not wait long enough to have their questions answered. The church wants to be powerful without the price. Listen next time you are around Christian royalty, a powerful man or woman of God. In the narrowed eyes and the low and humble voice they carry, you will see the road maps of much suffering, much ridicule, mocking, and back stabbing. What makes them different from others who have suffered the same thing? How they embraced their sufferings through forgiveness and did not try to arrange their prayers for their release, but rather they prayed for the release of those who hurt them. When I spend my time praying for those who hurt me, I don't have time to ask why. If I allow God to pressure my heart with the burden for my enemies, I begin to treat my enemies like only God can.

If I am careful to evaluate my life, I will see that at times the culture changes my view of God and I can become very hostile to Him and His ways. I tend to be a bit on edge with God and His methods when they go against the grain of my preferred individualism. When I ask the question "why?" what I am really asking is, "Why isn't God submitting to my way of doing things?" I can magnify my questions and thereby minimize God, or I can magnify my God who will always minimize my questions. The "why" of my life is often more about me than I care to admit. It is okay to ask questions, but not to demand an answer. Jesus cried out to his Father, "Why have you forsaken me?" As you remember, there was no answer. Sometimes my brain could not comprehend the explanation that God would give concerning any given moment anyway. The hardware of a computer will never be wiser than its creator. It can only operate within the parameters it has been given, and there is no frame of reference for the hardware to fully understand the mind of its maker or his thoughts. So it is with us. Faith does not keep us from asking the questions, it gives us the wisdom to wait for an answer when the rest of the world demands one now.

It's high time to sacrifice the idol of my humanity upon the cross of Jesus Christ. To know that the God of heaven sacrificed His life for mine should give me a comfort that even though I may not understand God, I have experienced Him, and experiencing love is always greater than defining it.

Chapter Ten

Finding the Place of Forgiveness

Failure comes in many shapes and sizes, yet its effects are always the same. We, in those failing moments, find it difficult to go on, difficult to open up, to relate to those who we see as a success. So, to connect we invent smiles from our storehouse of pain and we fabricate facades of success from our hearts' overflowing helplessness. These inner emotions seem to suck all the breath out of us like being swallowed by the ocean itself. When we feel this way, we feel guilty, and we are. But because we have the knowledge of guilt, it is almost impossible for us to receive the forgiveness from ourselves. Many have an easier time receiving forgiveness from God than they do from their own person. Yet God requires us to love ourselves, not in the selfish idolatrous way where we put ourselves before anyone else, but in the Christ-like way of having a love for ourselves that is equal to the love God has for us. Since this seems so foreign to us, we often dismiss it as an impossibility.

So we're caught. We are stuck in the middle of a Christianity where God has freed us, and of this we boast, yet we still hold ourselves in chains. One part of us feels free and the other part tormented. It is because we have not surrendered to God our view of ourselves. We still hold this as a right that we refuse to release. We have come to the place where we allow God to touch every area of our lives except our ability to self-punish. If you have never been here before, I question whether you have really been broken or not. This is a common place for humanity to tread, though it is a terrible and confusing place. Nothing makes sense here, nothing seems to work, and it only seems like a distant dream to escape, and all the while the reality of the gnawing hatred that we have for ourselves continues to thrive in our bellies.

We hardly feel worthy of God's forgiveness, let alone our own. But this we must understand: if we do not release what God has released, then it stays bound. Whatsoever you bind on earth will be bound in heaven, whatsoever you loose on earth will be loosed in heaven.

(Matthew 18:18) Through the un-forgiveness of others or our own selves, we bind what God has loosed. In this case we can only expect more failure. How can a runner run with only one leg free? How can a heart beat with one piece bound? How can a Christian be a Christian holding captive what God loosed? How can we be like Christ when we are not willing to do that which Christ has done? Like forgive ourselves?

As a pastor, there is one thing that I have seen in just about every person that I meet with or counsel. Somewhere in their life there has been a failure, and if it was large enough there also is a degree of self-hate. Christians at times are very sadistic people. Self-mutilation seems to give a temporary comfort to the ease the crimes we have committed. What we fail to realize in a personal way is that the cross is brutal enough, God does not need us to add to it. Jesus took your punishment, let Him keep it.

I find that it is easier to tell someone else to forgive themselves, but when it comes to doing it myself, I am more willing to let someone else off the hook than I am myself. Jesus said, "Do unto others as you would have them do unto you." (Luke 6:31) When I release others, I do so on the basis of love for Jesus and His commandment to me. Yet I also do so because I would have them do the same for me. So in a weird way, I desire for others to release and forgive me but I won't do it for myself. No wonder the world thinks we are crazy.

No matter how many times we try not to, we hold our lives to the comparison of what is not real. Sure, we could have done better in many areas of our lives, we could have made better choices and decisions that may have caused things to be different. But we didn't. We chose what we did. The current method that the church employs to deal with the past is to deny it, pretend it didn't happen, and utilize the forgiveness we asked for to erase the consequences as well. The blood of Jesus covers my sin, but not my consequences. A broken marriage may be mended in time, but it is not fixed immediately after we confess our sins. A father may repent of abandoning his children, but his repentance will never get back the years he lost with his kids. We may repent of our eating habits, but the blood of Jesus does not trim the unwanted fat from our waistlines as we kneel at the altar on Sunday morning. Forgiveness is the start of a new race, not the finish of an old one. Often we must go back and do our part to rectify that which was destroyed by our own failures.

Every now and then I allow my mind to wander into what might have been. I always come back with the same conclusion. If things would have gone the way I would have chosen for them to go, I would have never been exposed as the sinner that I was. My swollen pride would have blinded my eyes so that I would have only seen my good. Yes, if my life was what I hoped it to be, I would have, for the most part, forgotten God. I certainly would have never known the beggar's place in prayer as Jesus spoke about. I would have never known my Father who is able to meet my need where I could not. In my darkest pain, I have received my greatest revelations of who my Father is.

It is in the dark that I see His face the clearest, for that is when He is the closest to my broken heart.

The current American Christianity obscures the face of God more than any personal darkness can. How clear our Father made it to us that He loves broken hearts, and yet the whole of our lives are spent building castles of safety to ward off the effects of brokenness. The modern church highlights blessing, prosperity, safety, increase, and perfection, as if they were the goal of life itself. But sometimes these things rob the beautiful church of her ability to know the Jesus who painfully went through Gethsemane, and who in agony endured the cross. Within my lack I find God's abundance. It is not a wonder why Mother Teresa, Rich Mullins, Heidi

Baker, and a whole host of others live in a way that confuses the modern church. Finding God in broken surrender is finding the ability to forgive myself and all the things that I have done to others, myself, and my waistline. But also finding Him frees me in His strength to do what I could not do before. All of a sudden, my waistline is obedient to God where it was not before, I can make restitution where I used to only run, face the past I used to fear, and I can clean the mirror that I once covered with lies.

When we encounter the God who endured pain for our maimed souls, we are forced to look into eyes that do not condone or blame, they only offer forgiveness. When the miracle of being made into His image confronts the strongest parts of my brain, I am forced to bow to the reality that if He, whose image I am made in, can forgive me, then what is stopping me from forgiving myself? If God Himself does not condemn me, what right do I have to play the part of God by sadistically holding myself to some form of mental torment to pay for my crimes?

I remember reading the account of the crucifixion in Luke's gospel, on a day where I expected to receive no major revelation. When I got to the part where Peter denied Jesus, I noticed something that had previously escaped me. It said, "...and the Lord turned and looked at Peter..." (Luke 22:61) Like an arrow in the heart, I felt the weight of that moment. Peter didn't just deny Jesus in some closet somewhere. Imagine looking into the eyes of the man you denied immediately after you did it. I was rolling this around in my mind and I asked myself, what would I have expected to see in the eyes of a man whom I had just betrayed? Earthly men might convey a look of shock through their eyes, or pain, or anger, or unbelief. But what caused Peter to weep? It was in the eyes of Jesus that Peter saw forgiveness and love. Red handed, Peter stood guilty before the God of heaven and earth with denial fresh upon his lips, only for God to convey to him through His fiery eyes the forgiveness of heaven. This breaks the hardness of the human heart.

It took Peter getting close enough to the eyes of God to see that God did not blame him for his humanity. I believe it was this look that caused Peter to be able to return. He saw within the gaze of Jesus something beckoning him to return. The question I had to ask myself is, can I see those same eyes? Or have I fabricated God's gaze toward me to be something of disappointment and shame? Religion causes us to create God as He is not, son-ship forms us into the likeness of God as He is. Before I can be like Him, I must see Him as He is. I must look deep into His eyes and know that my failure is not bigger than His love and His precious blood. I must release my demented caricature of God that I created and worshiped for so many years.

There are times in our lives that our eyes are opened and we see clearly. Just like Peter did. Many times after we gain clear vision, a sickness settles in where faith used to reside. We feel deep sorrow because we openly see how we treated our Father. It hurts not because He is God, but because it finally makes sense what He did for me.

There is a story that goes something like this, "There was a blind girl who hated herself just because she was blind. She hated everyone, except her loving boyfriend. He was always there for her. She said that if she could only see the world, she would marry her boyfriend.

"One day, someone donated a pair of eyes to her and suddenly she could see everything, including her boyfriend! Her boyfriend asked her, 'Now that you can see the world, will you marry me?' The girl was shocked when she saw that her boyfriend was blind too, and refused to marry him. The boy walked away, and later he wrote a letter to her saying: 'Just take care of my eyes, I love you.'"

To see what God has really sacrificed for my freedom causes a deep sense of wonder and shame. But He expects me to use what He gave me. Forgiveness was freely given in the person of Jesus Christ and it is to be freely received by me. Am I arrogant enough to have God suffer the agonies of the cross willingly for me, only for me to turn around and tell Him that I will try to find another way to pay for my crimes?

It was the desire of God to heal Peter through Jesus Christ. Failure, real or imagined, is a wound that needs stitching. Though healed, it will always leave a scar.

Peter had failures and scars, but they were testimonies to the healing of God, which so infused itself into Peter's nature that even his shadow was affected by it. The healing of God knows no limits. Scars are the road maps of every Christian. These roads either lead you to the freedom of knowing healing or to the bitterness of only knowing bitterness and pain.

His blood sets me free from my sin, His blood releases me to forgive myself, but the blood does not take away the consequences that I must face. For this, He promises to be with me every step of the way. Allow the thoughts of God over you to flourish.

Jeremiah 29:11-13 "For I know the plans I have for you, declares the Lord, plans to prosper you and not to harm you, plans to give you hope and a future. Then you will call on me and come and pray to me, and I will listen to you. You will seek me and find me when you seek me with all your heart."

Chapter Eleven

Divorcing Fear

F ear usually ends up being a relationship. It is subtle but abusive. Scary, yet oddly attractive. If I allow fear to run my mind, I end up seeing peril in every situation, even if it's not really there. I also can't help but feel that I am the only one who can be in charge of these fearful situations that I see. Somehow I convince myself that I am somewhat of a savior if I am involved. Like, I alone have the power to stop them. Control is the human reaction to fear. Fear of failure leads to a deformed and warped attempt at trying to control God.

Job was a man whose heart stood strong before God. Daily offerings unto the Lord for both himself and his children seemed to ward off those things he was afraid of. On and on he performed his rituals unto his God, and

God protected him, until the day that God chose to deal with Job's fears. Job seemed to be in control of his life and his children's lives, but all that changed.

"That which Job feared came upon him..." (Job 3:25)

The fear of failure is in many ways worse than failing itself. Not because it is worse than failing, but because it often keeps us from ever trying. This is deadly when it concerns the great commission. It is easier for us not to join the team than it is for us to join and be the cause of the team's failures. Self-protection is a false comforter. It binds us to the "what if" of life while stealing from us the "what is" of life. Living in this way causes the constant worry of tomorrow to intrude upon the now. Like a vise in the mind, the fear of failing myself, my God, and my friends will eventually squeeze the charisma right out of my heart.

As I look back in my life, I think, "Why not be afraid of failure? After all, look at my track record." When I begin to judge myself by my past, I am no longer free to live in God's future for me. If I expect to fail, then I will not be able to have faith, to believe, to exert the energy and spunk that the situation requires. Like a zombie, I will march on with a plastic smile in a plastic world. Francis Chan, the talented author of "Crazy Love," said, "Our greatest fear should not be of failure but of succeeding at things in life that don't really matter." I find in my life that when success becomes about feeding the beast within, it matters not how successful I am if I am only creating something that will end up destroying me. The fear of failure is unfounded. "What does it profit a man if he gain the whole world and then lose his soul?" (Mark 8:36) Failure just reminds you that you are gloriously human.

I have spoken with many people who are afraid of their pasts. They seem to think of the past as if it's a mugger lurking around every corner, waiting to pounce on them once again. Or many people just view the past as the past and continue to choose the same things in life, all the while continuing to fail. These people, though, do not need this book, they do not even see that they are failures yet. Life has not fallen apart for them. But to those who see their past as a judgment upon their current standing, there is much hope.

You cannot counsel away fear. I've tried. Fear is a powerful force that is not eradicated by the mind, nor by understanding it, nor by knowing how evil it can be. No, fear is only expelled by love. And love cannot be understood, it can only be given or received. I must understand that God does not exist to keep bad things from happening, He exists for His glory, which is our pleasure.

Like many things in Christianity, the love of God, shown upon the cross of Jesus, has had its teeth pulled by our lazy and common use of it. The average Christian can tell you about the cross, yet its impact has been deadened due to a lack of heart and respect for what happened on that terribly awesome day. Few seasoned Christians can still weep at the vast enormity of God's love showed to us upon the cross. Words like grace, wisdom, love, and peace, all seem to categorize themselves into a personal definition that may or may not be full of power. These words have deviated away from the original authority that God showed the world through the cross of His dear Son Jesus. Allow me for a moment to tear off the religious overlay that we have applied to the cross of Jesus Christ.

God coming to the earth was God coming to face His enemies. Not the devil, not demonic forces of hell, no, He came to square off with us. His victory over hell was already secured by Him being God, but the victory over our hearts is why He came. He came to look into our eyes, to live amongst us, to understand, to put His arm around us, to learn of our pains and sorrows, and to be as we were intended to be. Yet God, in the form of Jesus, came undercover. No major announcement, only a few shepherds heard the news. If God were to come the

144

way I thought He should, would He not show the whole world? No, a couple of rag tag shepherds who took care of some dirty sheep were the only ones God allowed to see the theatrical entrance of heaven. The rest of the world lay asleep in ignorance. Much the same today.

When Jesus faced us, He saw deep into our hearts and saw fear. He saw people carrying the burden of facing God and all His holiness, yet also knowing they did not have the power to do what this God commanded of them. Jesus stared into the face of those who were slaves to the harsh dictatorship of the law. He watched "God-loving Jews" and Gentiles go home and beat themselves to oblivion because of their daily failures, the heart issues that they could not change, and their broken families that they could not fix. He saw the poor, those covered in fleas and lice as they lay in the streets. He lived with blue collar proselytes who fought hard to make enough money to pay their taxes and put food on the table. He watched men He created curse Him and His Father because of the pain they lived in. He heard the cries of a praying mother at night due to her sickened child. He listened to the songs of deliverance that His people would sing to celebrate the coming Messiah. Jesus watched and hated the arrogance that religion displayed and what it had done to

His people. He despised the current order of the church and the abuse of the law. It was against this backdrop that Jesus came as the "Man of Sorrows." This backdrop is also often found in the human heart.

This Jesus cried a lot. (Is 53:3) Maybe His disciples didn't see it, but the angels did. My question is: What made Him mourn? If I am honest, I will see that it was me. It was you. It was us. He came face to face with what causes us to fail, and He hated what it was doing to us. Like a mother watching the torture of her child, His tears marked His face and His heart cried in agony to change it. He really did love His enemies. Like a bride who cheated upon her husband with a thousand lovers, we burned the heart of a loving God. His response? He died to pay for our release from the law and former lovers that shackled our hearts.

It is one thing to know that Jesus died for my sins, it is quite another to know that Jesus died for me. Hearing that God died for my sins makes it as common as hearing that God is just paying off my overspent charge card. But to see that He died because He wants me, longs for me, aches for my heart and continually prays for my release, is quite another thing. To admit that God wants me is also to admit that God knows everything about me, too. Why would He want me in all that I have become?

Why would He care about my self-infested heart? Why would my enemy come all the way down here just to release me from the war I was in with Him? Why would He chase me down and overtake me when all I did was abandon, curse, and run from Him?

When God sent Jesus, God pursued the poor of the earth. Is it hard to understand that His only desire is to heal, to forgive, to release, to bless, to teach, and to love us? We do not feel worthy of this kind of pursuit because of our past, and because of our failures. Many times we refuse this love, knowing we need it, yet we are unable to humble ourselves to come to Him and take this free gift.

When Jesus came to this earth, He could have chosen His method of death. He could have put in for the Roman execution of beheading. He still would have died and the end result would have been the same. (Except for some prophesies, which He could have prophesied differently if He had wanted to.) But He didn't. Jesus personally chose execution upon a cross. The most feared instrument of death at the time; Jesus accepted what men feared. It was upon that cross, that the fear of death, the fear of loss, the fear of failure, and pain, were eradicated. He willingly chose to die and look like a failure in every area that we run from. He did this so that we could be free from what we fear. It was His love that drove Him to this choice. The teary nights in prayer, the agonizing heart under the weight of the world, the bleeding from His pores, and the petitions made to God in Gethsemane, were all forcefully driven by the love that He had for a liar like me. He did for me what I would not have done for Him. Perfect love cast out fear. (1 John. 4:8) Perfect love is not seen until a man is willing to lay His life down for His friends. (John. 15:13) It was this laying down of life that caused us to be shocked into reality by the depth of the love of God. I was His enemy, but He called me friend. I looked more like Judas than Jesus and that did not deter His love.

I had heard one time that if Jesus were to be beaten as many times as He was, that afterwards, from the backside, you would be able to see his intestines. After pulling out all of His facial hair, His face would have begun to bleed, leak fluid, and swell. The expansion of the skin around the thorns pushed into His skull would have caused an intense, fiery pain and an extreme blood loss would have ruined His ability to see what was coming next. The salt from His own blood burned His eyes, the same eyes He was trying to use to tell me that He loved me. The places where the Romans chose to put the nails intercepted with tender nerves in the wrists and feet, causing shock waves of pain throughout His entire body. The lack of water and sleep deprivation would have only fatigued His bloodied body even more and added to the excruciation. On top of all of this He had no one, complete loneliness. No companions to comfort Him in death. His mind reeled in the battle with doubt as to whether He did right enough to win us back. Hordes of demons encircled Him on the cross as if they were vultures waiting for His death. We all left Him when He was just like this, like cowards trying to save their own skins, we marched on in denial. I'm sure that if I were there I would have been shouting, "Crucify Him!" with everyone else. He was forced to endure this alone. Mocking crowds of self-proclaimed saints, human saliva being spit into the wounds of an all-loving God, rocks and dirt were thrown by the children of Abraham that He created, and Jesus was stripped naked before all the world. Yes, God was relieved of His dignity by the hands of His creation, and we seemed very justified in doing it.

Six hours He hung between heaven and earth, as a dying mediator before the great Judge of heaven, seeking to release His enemies from their crimes. He cried out for our forgiveness, He cried out to God to forgive our failure and to forgive our murdering His only Son. He laid the seal of life over our deadly sins and declared that it was finished. No more would the devil be able to boast that he owned the power of death and sin. No more would he be able to hang over the heads of God's people their pasts and failures. No more would he be able to be the superior being in relation to humanity. We were now free to file for divorce. Yes, this blood of Jesus washed and transformed the marital contract that I made with hell into a blank page.

The question becomes, "Why did He do this? Why does He love people with such enormous capacity to hate?" I don't know. There is no theology that can teach God enough to unpack this to the mind of man. The reason I don't know is because love is crazy, it is not able to be understood, love is God. Love is mad and reckless. It rivals the definition of insanity. God's love is beyond human ability, but not beyond human capacity. Strangely, God fits very well in my small human heart.

When I can rejoice that He loves me, I have received the fullness of the revelation of love. I need nothing more than acceptance, and I can have that in the fullness in the love of God. I know that I am alive when I can run and skip in the same fields where I used to cry and groan. God's love restores my ability to live, to succeed in Him, and to be a giver the way He loved and gave to the world. Love does not count the cost, it frankly doesn't care. What price is too high for ultimate love? All the world sold for its highest value would only be a mockery and insult to the true value of love.

So, I see that understanding is not the key to my freedom from being afraid. It is my acceptance of the love of a God, who is quite mad about me. When this love pierces my heart, I no longer have the capacity to consider fear or failure. It's simply not possible. I do not seek to fail my God, or my love for Him, so therefore I can be confident that love will endure and continue to conquer my fears.

In the great courtroom of God, I have filed my divorce papers. The marriage is over. The suffering complete. I am free from a relationship with fear and free to enter a marital covenant of love. I don't have to control things anymore. I just let Him be God, a God who has always been in control. Job finally figured this out. In Job's end he had more than his beginning. So it is with the Church. Once we let go of fear and control, our hands are finally empty to receive what God has always wanted to give us but could not. True Love.

Will you let go? Will you just take a moment and lower the walls and let God in? Will you repent (change the way you think) about failure? Will you stop offering your sacrifices of fear like Job did and just reach out and trust the love of a perfect Father?

I did. Friend, let me tell you, it is amazing.

Chapter Twelve

No Failure in Heaven

There was once an old Christian who spent years being tortured for his faith. For a long time, he endured agonizing cruelty. After his release, he was asked, "How did you endure the torture?" He said, "I will tell you how to endure being tortured for Jesus. You must see what you are going through as already being over. My power lies in the fact that I can live in a realm that is not yet present."

Paul wrote to us about this powerfully unpracticed principle. Ephesians 2:6 tells us that we are raised with Christ and seated in heavenly places. I was thinking one day and was astounded at the thought that, eternally speaking, I am not a body. Eternally speaking, I am not my failures, my circumstances, my emotions, or my shortcomings. Eternally speaking, I am a spirit. The same Spirit that raised Christ from the dead resides in me both eternally and now. As my mind swelled around this thought, I realized that I am already in heaven. I have already finished my course. In God's mind, there is no time, He exists outside of time and therefore He has already witnessed my end. He has placed me in the winner's circle before I have even finished the race. Therefore, what is real in heaven is what is real here, and likewise if it does not exist in heaven it really does not exist here. All my failures have already been washed away. There is no failure in heaven, therefore there is not really any failure here either.

I began to practice this kind of faith in small areas of my life to see if they worked. I began to believe I was already through my "torture." I began to grab ahold of my victory even while I felt like I was losing. A strange thing began to happen. Many of my trials did not change immediately, but I seemed to be undergoing a magnificent transformation. It was here that I found the truth that James spoke of when he said in Chapter 1:2, "Rejoice in trials and tribulations..." Before when I read this passage, I just assumed that all the disciples were a bit mental. But later on I found the treasure of joy buried deep in the mountain of trial. Being happy in God does not depend upon God changing our circumstances, but in Him changing us. After all, we are the biggest source of our own unhappiness. How many times do we finally receive those things that we felt would satisfy us and they ended up leaving us more hollow than before? My kids get so excited when they finally receive a gift they have been waiting weeks to get, and within a day or two it is left out in the graveyard of unused toys. Earthly things are empty. What we crave is a heart that has been completed, a mind that has been renewed, and an emotional makeup that is not blown to and fro by every unforeseen circumstance. We want stability.

Just as Jesus was crucified before the foundation of the world, all things of this world were already conquered. When I rest in my victory through the cross of Christ, I can find a reason to move forward and face giants that seem undefeatable. When I continue to live this way, I become a threat to hell itself. If there is nothing on this earth that can move me, then there is nothing that the devil can use to manipulate me.

All that is in the world is the lust of the flesh, lust of the eyes, and the pride of life. (1 John 2:6) These things do not exist in eternity where you and I do. When my eyes are on eternity, then temptation has lost its ammunition and the devil holds an empty gun. If I see this clearly I can agree with God, where before all I agreed with was a fallen, emotion-based, and corrupt world.

Mental conditioning is a powerful tool to the Christian. The Bible says that we have the mind of Christ. (1 Cor. 2:16) It does not say that, "You will one day get the mind of Christ." To know that I already possess what gave Jesus the edge over His enemy is an amazing and exciting thought.

I remember a story of a young boy who asked for a specific present for Christmas from his grandmother, who lived in another state. The boy was excited when he learned that his grandmother had agreed to the gift and would be sending it in the mail. Christmas came and went with no sign of the gift. The boy's mother said, "Maybe you should write Grandma a letter?" So, with much determination he wrote, "Dear Grandma, thank you so much for my gift, I cannot wait to play with it! Love, your Grandson." The little boy was not disheartened by the lack of the gift in person, he knew it was coming. After three more letters like it, the gift finally arrived. There was a letter attached, "Dear Grandson, thank you for believing me. I sent for your gift the moment I knew that you wanted it, but it was backordered from the company and I just now received it to send it to you. I hope you enjoy your present. Love, Grandma." The gifts that God gives may not seem to be in our hands, but as true as the air we breathe, they are in our hearts. Waiting for God to be God does not stop Him from following through on His promises.

We must learn to live in eternity before it arrives. It is impossible to judge and condemn my brother for his problems if I view things with God's eternal eyes. If my stains have been washed away, then there is that same grace that already abides on the head of my enemies. I can either help them access it or stomp around mad, thinking that they don't deserve the chance. In this case I am the man in the story who was forgiven a great debt and required a few pennies from my neighbor. All the answers to life are found when we view things from God's perspective. We may not get the answer right away, but it is there. Those who have been abused, raped, molested, beaten, rejected, mocked, and despised, they may feel like there is no hope. They may feel as if this world has swallowed up all purpose that they may have had. But in eternity their tears have already been wiped away, healing has already been applied. To know that God cares is sometimes enough to spark the fire of faith again.

How I view who I am determines how I fight when the battle arises. If I can apprehend the reality in my heart that I am already made into the likeness of Jesus Christ, then I do not need to spend the rest of my life seeking something I already have. I can spend the rest of my life activating what I have received. This is the difference between average Christianity and true son-ship.

The disciples before the cross of Jesus lived as if they were trying to achieve something, but after Pentecost they lived as if they had already received it. The power of God was always theirs, they just had to walk through the process to be ready to use it. Through much tribulation, we must enter the kingdom of God. (Acts 14:22) This is not just heaven, this is accessing what is in heaven for the now. It's giving birth, it hurts, it is not desirable, but the new life we bring forth is a wonder and awe to those around us. When we birth the kingdom within us it gives us a new hope to live for, a purpose that cannot be thwarted. Just as a mother finds a new purpose to defend and protect her baby, the church finds her purpose when she births this kingdom of God, often through some degree of suffering.

A Christianity that focuses my life only upon what is on this earth is a powerless religion. Faith is not so that we can polish ourselves to a certain degree of moral purity and then die. Our son-ship was given to expand the family of God, not worry about our reflection. Yes, we will go through hardships, and sometimes in these afflictions we will not act as we wish we would have, but this does not stop us from being sons of God. It only expands our vison of where we need to grow and learn. What we do is not who we are, we are spirits, sons of God. When this is righted in my mind, what I do flows out of who I am, not trying to change who I am by what I do. We are not allowed to define ourselves, God reserves that right, and through the Spirit of adoption He has already created the definition.

Eternally, you and I are sons of God. There is no improvement upon this title. I must harness and kill the desire in me to be better by doing. Obeying rules and laws does not make me holy. Most often it only makes me tired. I am liberated when I realize that sons naturally obey. If I find a lack of obedience in my life, I might want to start looking for the problem in the foundation of my set of beliefs. If I build my life doubting what God has said about me, then maybe I am tearing down what God is building in me just as fast as He builds it.

Sometimes it's scary to live outside of time. It seems like we are lying to ourselves about what is happening. When I start to think like this, I agree with my adversary quickly, but I also remind him of the other side of the coin, eternity. Eternity is where God and I are already sliding down the streets of gold in our socks. It's His house, His rules, and His kingdom. Believe me, He doesn't allow pain or the devil there.

We must understand that we do not possess God, He possesses us. It is His power in us that gives us the right to the inheritance of heaven. In his book, "100 Prison Meditations," Richard Wurmbrand tells of this truth. "The renowned tenor Caruso was obliged to sing in the opera on the day of his mother's death, in order not to disappoint the thousands of fans who had come especially to hear him. After the performance he exclaimed, 'I believed in the beginning that I had a voice; now I realize that the voice has me.'" ("100 Prison Meditations," ISBN 0-88264-180-8, pg 59) God holds us to Himself if we will allow it. In our beginning we feel as if we have faith. At the end, we begin to understand that faith has us. This is the shift of seeing with eternal eyes.

I get derailed from my faith when I ask God, "Why?" Usually there are no answers given to this question. When I place my future upon the altar of doubt and ask God why, I end up being the sacrifice.

There is a legend that says that Moses once sat near a well in meditation. A wayfarer stopped to drink from the well and when he did so, his purse fell from his girdle into the sand. The man departed. Shortly afterwards, another man passed near the well, saw the purse and picked it up. Later a third man stopped to satisfy his thirst and went to sleep in the shadow of the well. Meanwhile, the first man had discovered that his purse was missing and, assuming that he must have lost it at the well, returned, awoke the sleeper (who of course knew nothing) and demanded his money back. An argument followed, and irate, the first man slew the latter. Whereupon Moses said to God, "You see, therefore men do not believe in You. There is too much evil and injustice in the world. Why should the first man have lost his purse and then become a murderer? Why should the second have gotten a purse full of gold without having worked for it? The third was completely innocent. Why was he slain?"

God answered, "For once and only once, I will give you an explanation. I cannot do it at every step. The first man was a thief's son. The purse contained money stolen by his father from the father of the second, who, finding the purse, only found what was due him. The third was a murderer whose crime had never been served. In the future, believe that there is sense and righteousness in what transpires even when you do not understand."

Behind every temptation to ask "why?" is a God who holds the answer. We do not necessarily need the answer He holds, but we do need Him. Eternal vision is a cutting-edge weapon in the war of being human.

Rejoice that you are seated with Christ. Time will reveal all mysteries, but until then you and I are already wearing the victor's crown, and no longer do we bear the burden on failure.

So walk on, saint, move ahead and leave behind the things you long to be free from anyway. Embrace God's mind and heart about your life. Let go of the harsh words that have been spoken over you by others, and especially those spoken over you by yourself. Stretch your faith to believe that you are through your tears, through your pain, through your worries and struggles. Believe the bruised body of Jesus and its application to your wounds. The blood of Jesus beautifies failure, His blood made you human again, pure again, to believe again, to hope again, and smile again. You have been anointed by God with the divine blood of Jesus. You shared His cross and His resurrection, you share His power and His inheritance. You are no longer a failure, you are a son of God.

Welcome to the family!